THE

LIFE

THAT'S

WAITING

BRIANNA WIEST

THOUGHT CATALOG Books

THOUGHTCATALOG.COM

Copyright © 2025 Brianna Wiest.

All rights reserved. No part of this book may be reproduced or transmitted in any form or any means, electronic or mechanical, without prior written consent and permission from Thought Catalog.

Published by Thought Catalog Books, an imprint of Thought Catalog, a digital magazine owned and operated by The Thought & Expression Co. Inc., an independent media organization founded in 2010 and based in the United States of America. For stocking inquiries, contact stockists@shopcatalog.com.

Produced by Chris Lavergne and Noelle Beams
Art direction and design by KJ Parish
Circulation management by Isidoros Karamitopoulos
Author photo by Ashley Klassen

thoughtcatalog.com | shopcatalog.com

First Edition, Limited Edition Print
Printed in the United States of America

ISBN 978-1-965820-01-8

For my readers.

READ THIS WHEN...

You Can't Just Let Yourself Be Happy
15

Your Heart Is Breaking
And It Feels Like It Will Never Heal
27

You Don't Understand Why People Are So Unkind
41

You're Doing Everything Right
But Nothing Is Coming Together
47

You Don't Yet Have The Life You Want
53

You Don't Understand How Something That Once
Seemed So Meant For You Turned Out So Wrong
57

You Feel Like You'll Never Get
Past The Challenge In Front Of You
67

You Can't Stop Comparing Yourself To Others
73

You Want To Change Your Life
But You Don't Know Where To Start
87

You Care Too Much About What Other People Think
97

You Don't Feel Worthy Of Love
101

You Don't Know What You Want
109

You're Always Waiting For Something Bad To Happen
135

You Need To Let Go Though It Hurts To Do So
141

You Feel Completely Lost In Life
145

You Feel Alone And Don't Understand Why
149

You Don't Know What Your Purpose Is
169

You Aren't Sure You'll Find What's Meant For You
179

You Feel Misunderstood
183

You're Paralyzed By Fear
187

You Feel Like You Have To
Accept All Criticism In Order To Grow
197

You Don't Know Whether To Hold On Or Let Go
203

You've Lost Hope
209

You're Holding Yourself Back
213

You Don't Know What To Do Next
217

You Feel Like You're Hitting Your Upper Limit
221

You Feel Stuck Or As
Though Nothing Will Ever Change
225

You Feel Like Everything Is Falling Apart
233

FOREWORD

Brianna messages me from her house on top of a mountain in California, confiding in me that she is trying to conceive a book that could carry people while they navigate the most hopeful and the most hollow moments of life. She prefaces the message by saying that it's something she has been trying to transmute since she started writing many books ago, that the idea has always been a seed in her mind, that she has been fighting to alchemize it into existence. She proceeds to send me the most beautiful, unvarnished concept for a book called *The Life That's Waiting*.

She does this a lot—speaking hope into existence without realizing that she's in a channel of her own, talking about the things she wants to build, the things she hopes to see exist in this world, as if she's dancing with the words in her mind, as if all external noise has calmed, has quieted and she is in her own vacuum of creativity, her own atmosphere. It is an incredible thing to bear witness to—the inception of her genius, the small threads of thought that go on to become the books that impact the world in ways that change it.

This is the version of Brianna I am often gifted with. The friend. The artist. The voice piece to something greater, something protected, something that is rare and living inside of her.

However, to the outside world—Brianna is a different force. She is the person who has written nine books that millions of human beings have held with such tenderness. People look to her to help them make sense of their journeys in a way that is both wise and also pressing, a gentle but firm reminder that we often don't deserve the things that have happened to us, but that we owe it to ourselves to heal, to grow, to magnify our perception of ourselves, and therefore the possibilities that are accessible to us—the lives that are waiting for us on the other side of our discomfort.

And when we read these things, when they make impact with our souls, when they break through our exterior in a way that feels transformative, we often see the author as someone who is all-knowing, someone who has always had the answers. But the beautiful thing about Brianna is that she will be the first person to admit that she hasn't. She writes from a place of learning, rather than knowing. She writes the words she needed to hear when she was younger, the words she needed to hear when she was navigating doubt, when she was learning how to let go, when she was elbowing her way back into her heart, when she was redefining what it meant to hope, to trust, to love. And in this way, she conceives books that help for those who read them to do the same.

The Life That's Waiting is that kind of book. It will not give you a ten-step, measured list on how to become the person you hope to be. But it will hold your hand through the experiences that are shaping you. It will remind you, on your darkest days, on your most confused days, on the days that swell within your chest, that you are not alone. That someone else has walked this journey, that someone else has endured the same things, that someone else has made it through, has healed the hurt, has felt the fear. And it will act as a balm for whatever questions you have. An honest collection of words that you can turn to when you need a voice of reason, when you need a soft landing. A genuine collection of words you can turn to when you need to believe that the world has not forgotten you, that there is more to feel, that there is more to have faith in, that there is more to become, that there is a life that is waiting for you, that is reaching for you, on even your hardest days.

I know this book will inspire you to reach back.

I hope you do.

—Bianca Sparacino

INTRODUCTION

In her novel *Their Eyes Were Watching God,* Zora Neale Hurston said that there are "years that ask questions, and years that answer." If that is true, and I do very much believe it is, this book is the answer to a question I began asking myself many years ago.

This is the first idea I ever had for a book, and I had it long before I knew someone like me could even write books. I was 19 years old, and distinctly remember wishing that there was something that could act as a field guide to being human, like "an encyclopedia of feelings," as I phrased it back then. I remember wishing I had a companion guide to life, where someone could walk me through the things you don't always learn about in a formal way but that shape and inform your experience of being alive nonetheless.

Though I can't believe it took me this many years to finish this book, I also believe there's something important in the timing. This version is imbued with something I couldn't have accessed any sooner than I did. Through the process, I began to discover that the words were pouring out of some part of me that I didn't even know was there. As though I had been living out the answers for so many years—seeking, finding, and noting—and then finally putting the pieces together.

No matter what crossroads you may find yourself at, it is my sincerest hope that there will be something within this book that can act as a sort of anchor for you, a North Star directing you back toward what you know is true.

Because what I know for sure is that behind the life you are trying to hold together, on the other side of the life you are forcing to work…is the life that is waiting. The life that finds you when you let go of everything that's standing in its way. The life that's been there all along. The life that sustains itself, the life where things come together, and stay. The life that you know, deep down, is meant to be yours. The life that's always just one decision away.

If, on your way to it, you lose your direction—I hope you pick up these pages.

While you're reading them, I hope you take what helps and leave what doesn't, and let those untouched parts rest there for another person to find them, even if that person is you, someday down the road. I hope you tuck what you find into your back pocket, and if the hour ever comes when you are wondering what to do next, I hope that you discover you've already planted a seed back to your sanity.

More than anything, I hope you remember that I don't know anything. Listen only if the song I've sung to bring myself home is the one that reminds you of where yours may be.

Only if the things I tell myself are answers to the questions you didn't know you were asking.

Only if my voice sounds like the one you remember but haven't been able to find.

This is not my offering, this was just me trying to sweep the dust out of my house.

If it cleans yours too, you owe me nothing.

Live.

Do everything you've ever dreamed.

And if one day you find yourself on the shores of your new life, humming the song we learned to sing together…

Remember me.

And let me know how it is.

—Brianna Wiest

READ THIS WHEN YOU CAN'T JUST LET YOURSELF BE HAPPY

Happiness is not an epiphany, it's a practice.

As much as your conscious mind may tell you that it's all you want to feel, and as often as it tallies up and lists out all of the reasons for which you should already feel that way—all of the answered prayers, all of the opportunities, all of the facets of a genuinely good life that you logically know you have—the truth is that the subconscious mind, the greater piece of your inner working, wants to feel what is familiar.

You'd be surprised at what it considers familiar.

If you have spent years of your life on a healing journey, familiar is the breaking and the mending, the process of losing and finding, of ending and beginning. Familiar is healing, not being healed. If you have spent years of your life resolving the tension inside of you by solving other people's problems, by being the universal sounding board, the unpaid therapist, the person in everyone's life that becomes simultaneously responsible for them and their wellbeing and their future, familiar is the peace you find through changing what's outside of you, not what's within. Familiar is fixing, and fixing requires us to always see an issue, or to get very close to those who are likewise seeking a way to export their hurt onto a willing soul. If you have spent years of your life in fear, in lack, in a constant worry about what is next and whether or not you will be okay, familiar is uncertainty. Familiar is the state of acquiring and still not having acquired enough.

Mostly, if you have spent years of your life thinking that happiness is joyfulness—that high feeling you get when something truly tremendous is happening—then you have probably likewise spent all of the downtime between those peak states reaching, and wanting, and wondering why they are not more quickly and consistently arriving.

Familiar has become unhappiness, because you do not really understand what happiness is.

It's easy to think of happiness like a series of those highs that begin to cohere together into one consistent state, like stars that gradually fill the night sky until the darkness around them dissipates. In reality, happiness is what we often name openness, the ability to create, and be.

Happiness is being able to move throughout entire constellations of experiences, galaxies unknown and unseen, rather than just pinging back and forth between the familiar terrains. Happiness is the deep meaning we find in the life we are nurturing into form, in the people we are coming to be. It is where even the most routine and ordinary tasks begin to glimmer. It's found within the exploration, the trial and the error; and it is inhibited by the pressure or expectation that our first venture is our final path. The idea that if we do not get it right quickly, we will not get it right at all. Happiness is the strength to cry when things are beautiful and also hard. To grieve. To say how we feel, even when it scares us. Happiness is the fortitude to take everything as feedback and keep moving. It's not something we source from what's around us but rather the way we recalibrate the directives coming from within.

It's the way we learn to trust ourselves, to let our lives lay safely within the palms of our hands. To allow them to root, and sprout, and grow.

It's the way we begin to understand that the insatiable craving is not to have conquered the game but to stop playing it altogether; to withdraw our lives from the arena of the ego and to turn around into our own garden, and begin to build something beautiful.

What you are probably seeking is not the feeling of having arrived but the feeling that you can continue.

It is within the desire to get to the end of it all with a legacy left, a life fully lived that creates real meaning—and meaning? It's the thing that strengthens our resolve, our will. That weaves our story together, that gives us courage and faith.

Meaning is what allows us to endure the lows and accept the highs. Meaning is that quiet hunger to keep going. Meaning does not ask you to reach for the next level; meaning requires you to realize that the miracle is already in the room. Meaning does not want you to override discomfort in favor of sustaining a greater high; meaning asks you to embrace what's hard in pursuit of what's beautiful. Meaning is the way you love a child. Meaning is the way you look back at your life in decades from now and think—*I wish I'd tried harder, I wish I'd just gone for it.* Not because those things are simple, but because they are so clearly worth it.

A life of meaning is one where you wake up each day excited for what is to be created, to be experienced, to be felt. It's falling most deeply in love with the climb. It's the recognition that there is no destination but death. A life of meaning is where you see and understand that you are part of something greater than yourself. Yes, the peak states are incredible when they are found, but they are nobody's constant. When they are, we often tarnish our bodies and our minds. We are strengthened where we are challenged, we are grown where we are pushed to open up and move forward. We are here to create something, and that something is, firstly, our own selves. Those selves are the instruments through which we are able to play the song of our lives.

Meaning is not when we are able to avoid doing the dishes, but finding gratitude and peace in the productivity of having a home to care for in the first place.

Meaning is not what's taken but what's experienced within the virtue of giving.

The question that you are really meaning to ask yourself is, *what do I want my life to feel like in the most quietest and unassuming moments, and what am I willing to endure in order to create that sanctity of reality for myself?*

A life of meaning may feel like an absolutely impossible state to reach, as though a question so complex and so existential could not be easily or simply answered. But you already know what it is you want. It's the things you feel gently inspired to do each day. When those nudges get ignored for long enough, they harden into walls that are triggered when something presses up against them. That is why our greatest wounds often point to our deepest destinies—because they are the same place where we have the most compounded potential that's gone untouched.

Your meaning is the way you'd like to do your hair differently, and the project you have at work, and the way you organize the cabinets, and the friends you text, and the things you've signed up for, and the emails you have to answer, and the workout you keep missing, and how good it feels to do the simplest things of all—to wipe the countertops clean after a long and exhausting day, to lay down and to just breathe. Your meaning is the big love you know you're meant to find when you stop letting the little ones take up so much space. It's the passion you know you're meant to devote a significant part of your life to, the trips you know you're called to embark upon, the places you're meant to see and to know.

When you begin to see every one of those instances of inner knowing as tiny invitations to meaning, you begin to generate momentum. You get more and more inspired, because you feel more and more accomplished. You become more productive. Your capacity increases. You begin to see more opportunities and you begin to take them. You do this, again and again, for long enough, and you discover that you have changed your entire life. Rather than seeking the next milestone, the next bragging right, you began seeking the joy of tomorrow. You stopped trying to find happiness in an idea of how good things are, but in the lived, hour-to-hour experience of making them what you want them to be.

When you do not know what it is you want, you wait until your heart stumbles upon something simple, something easy.

You begin there.

You start where you are called, where you are moved. You begin with what you probably need most, which is rest, or quiet, or to nourish yourself well. When you accept that these small forms of healing are your first call to meaning, that is when the bigger picture can begin to emerge.

You begin to stretch your hopefulness out by milliseconds, at the beginning.

You begin by becoming aware of when you're getting pulled into an old emotional pattern, and you try your best not to project the inner tornado onto the outside world. You give yourself grace. You remind yourself that this is where you have found a sense of safety. That at least here, you know what's around the bend. You know how the breakdown goes, the spiral. It's a dance you could do in your sleep. It allows you to occupy time in a way that is natural and intuitive, because of course, it has become that way over time. When you build a new world around a raised baseline, you are called to constantly give yourself and others the benefit of the doubt. Not so that you are naive or blind; but so that you do not keep hooking the old stories into the new reality. So that you are able to open your eyes in the morning and see things as they actually are, clear from the way your history wants to color them, so that once again, you look outward and are familiar with what you see.

At the end of the day, the artist is just the one who kept painting. The writer is the one who kept letting the words form into sentences, into sentiments, into pages, into messages, into hope. The photographer is the one who kept capturing. The mother is the one who kept caring. The teacher is the one who kept learning and sharing. The leader is the one who kept braving the unknown and holding up a torch. The hero is the one who kept going, when anyone and everyone else would have given up entirely.

A life of real meaning is not one where we accomplish extraordinary feats, but one where we realize that those extraordinary feats are only reached by constant, ordinary acts. A life of real meaning—which is an *actual* life of deep happiness—is one in which we can see them as one in the same.

Happiness isn't found; it's forged. It's what we make ritual, what becomes routine. It's not luck, it's discipline. Plant where you want to root. It will be uncomfortable to break out of the seed either way.

READ THIS WHEN YOUR HEART IS BREAKING AND IT FEELS LIKE IT WILL NEVER HEAL

You are meant to get your heart broken. It is a universal experience, if you're brave enough to open your heart in the first place. You are meant to meet people throughout the course of your life with whom you connect deeply and to show one another things unseen, both about your own selves and each other and what it means to be together, and then you are meant to outgrow some of them. You are meant to set some of them free. You are meant to discover the threads that intertwine do not always connect at the ends. You are meant to learn from both the having and the losing.

I know that does not one single thing to alleviate the cold shock that's pummeling through your nervous system right now. I know it feels like every bone in your body has gone numb, like you're still stunned by the disconnect from something you once found so much hope in, so much home; and I want to tell you that while this hurts, it's also normal. We aren't meant to be ripped from the things we've grown attached to.

And if we are?

There is always a reason.

Often beyond what we can understand at the time.

Right now, you need to nurture and you need to express. You need to allow the experience to move through you, no matter how much it feels like your insides are banging around inside your body, asking for an outlet, for an answer that you cannot seem to find. You need to understand that the resolution you seek is also the foundation of the problem—that life is good but hard. That hurt is an inevitable part of the course.

Once you have emptied yourself out of all the inner chaos and you have returned back to a semblance of neutrality, you have a wide and shining opening. One that will shift your sense of possibility, purpose, and meaning. One that won't just get you to the other side of this, but that will allow you to actually use this as a springboard to the person you were meant to be, the life you were meant to lead.

You get to decide whether the losses of your life will be lows or inflection points that act as catalysts to your greatest self-investment. They are either periods through which you decide whether you will only endure life's valleys or in which you see clearly that life gets disrupted on the surface when something deeper and truer is attempting to emerge from beneath.

You get to decide if you see heartbreak as a facet of your own specific and individual unworthiness or as a painful but essential part of the growing process that most people endure at some time, if they are lucky enough to get to love in the first place.

You get to decide if getting it wrong gives what you need to know in order to finally get it right.

You get to choose how you're going to see it.

The losses outweigh the victories at the beginning of anything, but most especially in love. Unless you remain forever with the first person you fell for, the process will inevitably look like a string of disappointments until the right one finds you, until the right one fuses their life to yours, until the nucleus of your existence shifts to the two of you at the center, rather than just one.

There's more in the equation than just chemistry, or connection, or ease.

There's also the future.

There's also what's next.

There's the person you are but also the one you're becoming. The one you most want to be. There are the cities that have been waiting for you, the things that have your name on them, the ideas waiting to be born.

If you are like most people, you can reflect back on at least a few things you've lost in the past and recognize that you may even be grateful that some of them did not work out the way you once wanted them to. You did not know what you did not know. You could not see the picture in entirety. Who they'd become, and who you would—what once seemed so matched on the surface presented an entirely different story and reality just beneath.

Life knows.

Life has heard conversations you haven't.

It's seen things you haven't.

It knows things you don't.

When life is moving you in a direction that is in direct opposition to what is seemingly your heart's desire, you must find an inkling of surrender, of trust, of consideration that perhaps what seems like a denial is actually a prevention, a way of ensuring you arrive where you most need to be. Maybe this is actually the moment at which you realize life loves you so much, it will withhold what you are most ardently asking for to make sure you receive what you most wholly and completely deserve.

When it feels impossible to let go, as though you are gripping the pain by the throat and pulling it closer, please know that there is almost always another reason. There is almost always an ulterior motive. What you are losing is not just a companion, a flame, or a friend; it is also a sense of purpose, a sense of certainty, a sense of knowing what's next. What you are simultaneously mourning is your former idea of what life would be. If you don't build a new life in its place, please do not be surprised if the idea of the person you once knew and loved fills and consumes the emptiness.

That where you once placed someone so as to fill your future plans, in their absence, their ghost-form—even just the thought of them—will acclimate to taking up an equal, and sometimes greater, portion of your attention, your psyche.

If this is the case for you, then you must look at that open-ended new life as your golden horizon.

That is where you must set your attention, even in your hardest hours.

Because you cannot find your soulmate if you are not embodying your soul.

You cannot know who is right for you if you do not know what is right for yourself. From the abstract compatibility to the very practical ones, you cannot be properly matched to someone with whom you could realistically build a life if you are not yet clear on what you want your life to be.

This is your chance to revise that.

To open your eyes and see.

Sometimes, the things we hold onto most tightly are actually the ones that keep us safely situated on the shore, that seem to exalt and free us from the thing we often most truly fear, which is becoming who we are really meant to be. Braving the unknown and building. We think of loneliness as the absence of other people, when really it is the result of a disconnection from ourselves. We can be most lonely in a crowded room, most content all on our own.

This is not to say that you are meant to do life by yourself.

You aren't.

It is just to say that if you're in a window where you're more by yourself than you want to be and your efforts to branch outward aren't taking root the way you hoped they would, you are actually being given an offering, an opportunity, to befriend yourself more closely and more truly. It is from there that all the rest of your connections will be born.

Everyone is there for you on Friday night when life is easy and everything is exciting and everyone is looking for something to do. Everyone is there for you when circumstance places you beside one another, when the overlapping of your experiences is so close, it generates a sense of togetherness. Everyone is there for you when life is easy and the connection is effortless. The presence of strain is a test, and the relationships that endure are the ones we are meant for. The ones that don't aren't suited to carry you through the rest of your life, but do you know who needs to be?

You.

You are the one who wakes up with you on Sunday morning. You are the one who you take care of, day-in and day-out. You are the one making all of your executive decisions. You are the one filling the dead air, the open space. You are the one advocating for your needs and being vulnerable with your feelings. You are the one on every adventure. You are the one falling in love, and out, and back in again. You are the one you have to be with this entire time, and when you are no longer afraid of what it would be like not just to survive on your own but to dance even if you are by yourself, you discover something potent—the willingness to let go of the connections that you've held together out of fear and force. You are more free. You are not afraid of loss, of rejection. You are not hinging your comfort on whether or not someone else decides to stay.

Because even if all of your dreams come true and you are eternally surrounded by all of the people you love and who love you most—your life is still your own.

It's still you and you, until the very end.

Your willingness to embrace this rather than fight it is not only a sign of your strength, it's a sign that somewhere deep inside, you know that a life that is honest, even if less comfortable, is more worthwhile than one in which every doubt and fear is suffocated by false connection.

It might serve you at this juncture to make a list of all the reasons you might be kind of secretly glad your last relationship is behind you. All the things you quietly didn't like or feared you'd have to endure forever. Remembering your own dissent, the ways in which your quietest instincts are being affirmed and supported by this parting, helps to ease the louder parts that are asking to return to the familiar, to the sense of what could've been.

Because one of the hardest but truest lessons is that good things don't end.

Whether or not you are ready to see the nature and reality of your past relationship in totality is a matter of timing and processing, but when you are, you will most likely be able to identify all of the times the splintering, the fracturing, the revealing of incongruence, was evident and right in front of you. In a state of intense grief, it can feel as though everything you ever wanted and needed was pulled away from you. That is the regret—that you could not love that relationship into a deeper perfection. Part of your healing will encompass the recognition that what falls apart, what leaves, often does so for a reason. That the misalignments outweighed the places in which you connected.

A greater truth began to eclipse the illusion of the story you told yourself of how things should be.

This is actually life working in your favor.

The point is that you will get there, one day.

You will find your person, both where you least expect and where you always could have guessed.

You will find the person who enters your alone world and wants to be with you, even there. You will find someone who loves you with as much conviction as you do them. You will find someone who wants all of it, all of life with you. You will find someone with whom you see a future, and the virtue of all of that love will shine a bright light onto all of your fears—and that is when this inner work will become most evident.

Right now, you're deciding who is going to show up.

Will it be the version of you who has grown and become even more themselves through the hurt?

Or will it be the version who stayed wounded, who might risk losing the right thing all because an old version of them couldn't make the wrong one stay?

Trust that life loves you enough to break your heart if it means saving your soul.

READ THIS WHEN YOU DON'T UNDERSTAND WHY PEOPLE ARE SO UNKIND

People take on the characteristics of those who have most deeply hurt them. Within their unkindness, they are actually revealing to you the shape of their wound. What they have done to you says far more about them than it does about you.

Your choice becomes whether or not you will allow the shape of that wound to perimeter off your own peace; whether or not you will choose to engage it, inflame it, and over time, adopt it as your own. Your choice is whether or not you will allow those characteristics to impress themselves upon you, whether or not you will be a pattern-breaker or enter yourself into the karmic free-fall.

When you react, you concede.

You start playing by their rules and if you are not careful, you will begin living within them. They become you, indistinguishable from your former sense of self and truth. They become your framework, your safe zone. If you continue to engage, the perception of who you are allowed to be and what you are allowed to do will continue to shrink until it feels as though nothing is safe and there is nowhere to go.

This does not excuse another person's behavior toward you, it does not justify it or make it more whole. It is just the acknowledgement that you cannot control it or them, and so your work begins in your own arena. It is your response that will determine the nature of this moment, of this disruption, of this difficulty.

It is your response that will shape your life.

When someone sees another person living outside of the wound perimeter in which they are currently existing, their openness scratches the place where their hurt still sits. Their existence is bothersome, because it is a reminder. It is a reminder of all the ways they're living within the limitations, imagining that they would keep them safe.

Though of course, it only suffocates them further.

When those same people see others not abiding by their fears—the agreements they unconsciously made to play small—all of the repressed energy that's gone unused sometimes wells up and projects outward, when what it really wants to do is infuse inward and go forward.

What this moment is asking of you is that you become more capable of identifying when people are acting from their unconscious spaces and to choose not to level yourself in response. What this moment is asking of you is for you to start paying attention to your own responses and reactions, to also begin settling into the knowing that we often don't see people as they are, but as we are. Our filter and interpretation is a lens that adjusts over time. It shifts to match where we see ourselves.

Some people come into our lives to encourage us, to guide us, to be companions on the journey. Others come as reminders of the ways in which we have surrendered our autonomy, our power. Others come as reminders of who we might become if we do not change our ways. Others come to reflect the unseen parts of ourselves back to ourselves; and they, too, are guides in their own ways. Teachers.

Some people come into our lives just to show us who we do not want to be.

If you have come across one of them, please do not allow their jadedness to steal your kindness, your warmth. Please remain supple, open to the world and its offerings, its greater plan for you.

Please take this as a chance to decide you will not pick up more baggage just because someone else is carrying a heavier load. Please take this as a chance to firm up your boundaries, your resolve. Please take this as a moment to know that you do not owe anyone your grace, certainly not those who have been ungracious to you; but you do owe it to yourself.

You owe it to yourself to remain untouched by all the ways in which the world will attempt to harden you. You owe it to yourself to proceed.

You owe it to yourself to determine the kind of person you want to be and how that person will allow themselves to be treated. Not in the sense of declaring and fighting for their limits, but communicating them most effectively by what they will and will not engage with, what they will and will not enable.

That is what's in front of you at this most unlikely moment.

I hope you choose your peace.

●

Some people show you what's possible if you keep going, and others show you what's possible if you give up.

READ THIS WHEN YOU'RE DOING EVERYTHING RIGHT BUT NOTHING IS COMING TOGETHER

Sometimes, we don't get what we want because we are meant for things far greater than we'd ever let ourselves believe.

Sometimes, we fail not because we are lost or inept or in some other way lacking, but because some deeper knowing inside of us is beginning to take hold, and some greater vision is beginning to take shape, and instead of a life we can tolerate, we begin moving toward one we can't get enough of.

Instead of a consolation prize, we start preparing for the victory lap. Instead of believing that we are not enough because we could not thrive within what was not meant for us, we begin to realize that we are not meant to excel at a life that is not designed to make the most of who we most essentially are, what we most fundamentally love, what we are most inherently born to be.

You are not behind for the ways in which life did not turn out the way you once wanted it to. The gap between where you are and where you most want to be will be filled by the person you become—and that is why we have dreams in the first place. Not so that we might arrive somewhere that is perfect, but so that we will press up against the bounds that we think limit us and move beyond them. To see with crystalline clarity that we are limitless beyond even our own comprehension. That we are designed with the potential to fulfill what quietly inspires us, what motivates us, what interests us, what enlivens us, what awakens us in every sense.

We don't only have to grow, we also have to learn. We have to confront our shadows and our demons. We have to know the ways in which we are inclined to self-destruct. We have to understand what we do not want life to be before we can grasp what we do. Becoming the whole of who we are is not a matter of solely embodying the beautiful things in our hearts, but also befriending the hard ones.

We reside, always, at the edge of everything—all of the past behind us, and all of the potential in front, and all of the doorways around. The humbling, the losing, the stopping, the releasing, the slowing, and the stillness is just trying to give us the eyes to see.

You do not have to instruct a flower to bloom. You do not have to tell it how to root. You do not have to wish for it to sprout, you do not have to affirm that it will continue to reach toward the sun. You do not have to fear that it will not grow. You only have to arrange the environment so that growth is the inevitable outcome.

READ THIS WHEN YOU DON'T YET HAVE THE LIFE YOU WANT

A beautiful life is not stumbled upon, it is built. It is chosen. It is nurtured over the years. A beautiful life is made from the heart, not the head. It is not one we can rationalize our way into, it's one that must be felt. A beautiful life is not one that is immediately comfortable but one grown through the acknowledgement of what is worth being uncomfortable for. It is not one that is easy, it is one that is worth it.

A beautiful life is composed of the things our 90-year-old selves would have wished we'd done with the years in which we were so young but didn't realize, before the decades piled up and passed us by and we came to find how little time even the luckiest among us have. It is made of all the little whispered prayers they'd have for us as they looked back, the same way we imagine our younger selves now and wish we could impart and instill so much guidance, so often leaning in the direction of—go where your heart already calls you, move toward the truth you already know.

A beautiful life is made with someone who not only makes you fall in love with them but makes you fall in love with the person you become because of them. The kind of human being they push and inspire you to be. The kind of person who loves you as you are while still holding space for your growth. The kind who would carry you down the steps if you could not walk anymore, who would hold your hand until the last minute of the last hour, with whom you could have nothing but it would still feel like everything.

Happiness is not how your life appears, it is the quality of your connection to it. How deeply and intimately those bonds run. How much you truly cared about what you were doing and the people around you and the memories you made and how bravely you put your heart into your days, rather than hiding yourself away and wondering if you could make things appear full on the surface, while it all sits empty just beneath.

•

Your ability to create resides in the millisecond that is right in front of you. The more time you spend fixated on what's way behind or far ahead, the more you surrender your power. More of your life slips away.

READ THIS WHEN YOU DON'T UNDERSTAND HOW SOMETHING THAT ONCE SEEMED SO MEANT FOR YOU TURNED OUT SO WRONG

When we think of what is meant for us, what is right, it often seems like a finality; a landing place upon which we will construct the foundation of who we will become. When we think of what is meant for us, we often imagine that if we could just make the correct connections between the stars, we'd get them to align, and then there would be nothing else to calculate, nothing more to solve. We'd find where we are meant to be, and then we'd simply arrive, and be.

It is as though we imagine the things that are meant for us are ways of escaping the unknown or the unpredictable. In place of a life wide-open, we get one walled off in just the right dimensions. With the perimeter of our canvas defined, we feel safe enough to create. To begin.

That is why it can feel so upending, so debilitating, to lose what we were once so sure of. To have our intuition questioned in such a way, to realize we were so wrong. To discover that the little inklings that led us down a certain path or to a particular person were seemingly leading us astray. That the place in which we once imagined we'd be growing a future has now become the ground zero upon which we must muster up the fortitude and resolve to keep going and keep seeking to rebuild our lives. But the inner drive has diminished, because we cannot trust where we are bringing ourselves, we do not know what is real.

The idea that there's just one thing out there that's right for us denies us the beautiful nuance of what life really is. It gives us an experience that is one-dimensional, when it has the capacity to be so much more.

There are many different soulmates for each phase of our soul's evolution—in love, in work, in home, in any way you may imagine yourself finding what is right, and landing. At each phase, a variety of right things could come in and color the chapter in different ways. Some may be more preferable than others; some more aligned with our pre-established notions and concepts of what we thought life might be. But ultimately, we come to find that the things that are actually right for us are not the ones we choose and then continue to have them stay right by the virtue of us having decided that they are. They are the things that we can grow alongside and further into. The things we can grow with.

It is the openness, the willingness, the ability, to grow alongside one another that defines and determines what remains right for you.

And if we come to a fork in the road where the growth is no longer congruent, where your eyes are set in directions too different to keep walking alongside each other, to justify or make sense of remaining where you are or as you are, then the final act of love is to set yourself free to find the life that is calling more strongly. To allow the old house to become someone else's new home. To place down our work so someone else can pick it up. To free our love to find someone who can meet them in the moment, as they are now.

You did not get it wrong.

No, you did not make a mistake.

You stumbled into just the person who would let you experience love at the level at which you were. You discovered that you could make a home in many houses; that no matter what you had to offer, there were others out there who needed to receive what you could create, what you could give. And that when it was time to let go of what was, the next thing would always catch you. The road would always rise.

How beautiful, to think that you were given the chance to know love not as only the final and most perfect versions of yourself, but other ones along the way, too. How beautiful, to think that you were able to know home not just as the final place you would ever exist, but in little alcoves, in little corners, in little flats and apartments and all the things that held you along the way. How beautiful, to realize that the world would be so eager to meet you no matter how you showed up, just as long as you did. And how beautiful, that when you had outgrown what you'd once been a match for, life would not allow you to settle or to stagnate. That love would continue to pull you toward ever-brighter and more expansive horizons.

Yes, the way you once saw something or someone may have changed.

It may have changed faster than you ever anticipated that it could or in ways that you never would have imagined that it might. But that does not lessen and does not negate what you thought you knew at the beginning, what you imagined that you saw. You *were* right—it was the next step, even if it was not the last step. There was something within that experience that you had to learn, needed to know—even if you are still uncovering what that is, even if you are still piecing together the clarity.

More importantly than anything else, the fact that you see differently now, that things feel altered in some way, means that you have grown. You have shifted, you have changed. Though there may still be some younger parts of you gripping onto the old dreams and what was once so familiar, there's a stronger part of you saying—let go. There is something more waiting. Love does not just come in one person, one place, or one form.

So if you are gazing toward the future and you do not know what to do, please remember that no matter what you choose and no matter where you go—life will meet you there. It will meet you because it is within you, because it is you.

If you have the courage to brave a bit more uncertainty than the rest, you will come to find and know that it's never about whether or not one thing is the right decision. It's not: *can this be the most right and final decision I will ever make?* But rather: *What further decisions could this one lead me to? What experiences, what choices, what realities, what people? What kind of person would I inevitably become by the virtue of allowing this into my life, by choosing it, by devoting myself to it even through the hard patches? Who would I become if I loved most fully, if I experienced this most completely? Where is this going? Where does it lead? What is here? What might be?*

You'll come to find that what we often refer to as a "wrong" decision is just one that lacked any further mutual growth potential. The final lesson was what it was to let go—how we came to accept that it just wasn't meant to carry us forever, as few things are or do.

It's a trick of the mind to assume that you are meant to just get it right once and then place down your ambition and allow life to occur without your participation. It robs you of what is possible, what is inside. Instead of thinking that you are endlessly and irreparably lost because you are still in the process of turning the page between the chapters of your life, please consider that you've arrived at more of a completion point than not.

There is more of you ready to leap than what is willing to stay. And that, itself, is a victory. That is something to appreciate.

Because the more you come to know, and embrace, and nurture, and build yourself more coherently and completely—the things that are that much more right for you *will find you.*

And one day you will look back, cradled within a life more beautiful than you thought could be true, and know that what got you there was every step along the way.

Even steps backward are part of the dance. Trust that something vital was learned and found within these experiences. Trust that something crucial came to be.

READ THIS WHEN YOU FEEL LIKE YOU'LL NEVER GET PAST THE CHALLENGE IN FRONT OF YOU

There are anxieties you had a year ago that you did not even think of today. At some point, you consider your fear for the last time, and it leaves. But if, in its place, a mental container continues to exist, you will find a way to fill it. You will always be able to take what is around you and twist it into that shape, you will always be able to make something appear as that form. You will always be able to find what is not going for you. You will always be able to find something to worry about, something to focus on that slowly weathers your resolve and brings you right back down into what you've always known.

And so your job right now is to break down the walls of that container and rebuild. Your job is to confront the limitations that hold it in place and defy them. Your job is to build a life beyond those former confines so as to render them irrelevant. When life gives you a lesson, it is not giving you a punishment. It's giving you an opportunity to embody the qualities of the person you have always wanted to be, not just so that the challenge in front of you transforms, but so that everything else does, too.

One day, you will think about this worry for the last time. One day, you will feel that hot wave of grief roll over you one last time and the intensity will not repeat itself. It will lessen and loosen its grip. One day, you will allow yourself to be held back for the last time—and you will not know it is the last. Eventually, your memories will hollow themselves, they will neutralize. You will be able to recall the past without being pulled back into it. You will be able to tell your story of your life without feeling as though you cannot keep writing it freely.

You will let go.

You will let go without even realizing that you are doing so, but it will only happen when you stop trying to place one thing behind you, and start picking something better up in its place.

There is a time for everything. There is a time to receive and a time to release. There is a time to know and a time to question. There is a time to grieve and there is a time to grow. And this moment might not be the threshold where that growth point begins, but it's most likely a moment that's leading to it. It's most likely a moment where the seeds are being planted as what's overgrown is being weeded. In this hour, you are figuring out who and what you're going to cultivate.

The discernment period is as important as the planting, as the nurturing. This kind of mental clarity is only born of the times in which we are forced to sit with ourselves, look more deeply, and emerge with a greater truth. This moment is not in vain, it is not being wasted. You are picking up the pieces of what you're about to become. You're dwelling in the twilight of what's about to dawn for you.

You're making certain of what you'd like the rest of your life to be.

You aren't being asked to just get past this moment, to only endure. You're being asked to transform through it. Life is giving you a chance to swell to a wholeness greater than you previously conceived. Say thank you.

READ THIS WHEN YOU CAN'T STOP COMPARING YOURSELF TO OTHERS

When your comparisons of yourself to others are obliterating your confidence, infusing a sense of worthlessness and helplessness deep inside you, making you feel as though you are and always will be falling behind, what you must realize is that you are currently on the losing end of a game that once allowed you to win.

When we engage in comparison, it never just goes one way. We are never able to simply hold our own virtues up against someone else's vices and feel affirmed for how much lighter, how much better, how much more bearable our humanity is than theirs. Eventually, the tables we invented turn on themselves. Someone who we perceive to be farther ahead of us comes along, and all of a sudden, all of the validation we found in the way we placed ourselves in life dissipates. We realize that the hierarchy—the centermost platform of the podium upon which we thought we stood—existed solely within our imagination. Where we once found comfort, we now find ourselves crushed.

If you think it is a competition, you have already lost.

Comparing is the way that we source a sense of self when we otherwise lack it. It is an inauthentic way to fuel ourselves emotionally. When we have no real gauge on how fulfilled we are, how content, we rely on how we are doing in relation to others to give it to us. This, of course, is really just another way of superimposing someone else's mind over our own. It's a way of seeing life through another person's eyes rather than feeling it through our own hearts. Because in the imaginary comparison game, there's always a judge, and it's never us. We are always at the whim and the mercy of how we project that we are perceived. When we are not firm within the real, grounded, lived experience we are having, we conflate that perception for our reality.

The happier you are with your own life, the less you need other people to be.

What's really emerging is not the recognition that you're not good enough because someone is better, but that you are actually not fulfilled enough by your own experience—and you can no longer fake it anymore.

When your life is really enough for you, your mind does not jump to comparisons in the first place. There's just no impetus to initiate such a thought process. You're so immersed in the experience that you're having, you have no need to generate a better feeling about it by imagining how it would be perceived. Your own experience becomes enough—more than enough. You realize that you were never meant to be playing a game in the first place, and that the premise of the competition in and of itself is flawed and non-existent. The things, the people, and the joys that you are meant for are unique to you. The things, the people, and the joys that are meant for someone else are unique to them. There is no cross-over in fate, in destiny. We are not awarded what's ours because we have proven ourselves to be more deserving of it than someone else. We only arrive at such a mindset when we are fighting for someone else's life.

When you are ready to lay down your arms, you will realize that it is time to begin fighting for something else.

Your own.

You don't want to be better than another person, you want to be enough for yourself. You want your life to actually feel as though it is being lived. You want to feel love radiate out from the middle of your chest, and to receive it back. You want connection. You want to feel at ease in your own skin. You want to feel settled into yourself, into the things you are meant to do, into the things that allow you to fall asleep at night, finally feeling at peace, because you lived in integrity, because you did what you came here to do.

That journey is not an easy one to embark upon. It requires the unearthing of your soul beneath the layers of ego that have hid it so well, kept it safe from being bruised. It requires the ultimate remembrance that such damage is impossible, that spark within you is evergreen. It requires you to be vulnerable, to feel the complete range of your human emotions—not just the good ones but the hard ones, too. Most of all, it requires you to finally accept the ways in which you are not happy with yourself, and to stop using the image of how well you imagine others may see you as doing to act as a coverup for that hollow emptiness lingering just beneath.

You have to be brave now.

You have to fill your life with what matters to you, even if it doesn't make sense to anyone else. You have to be honest. You have to heal. You have to clean up your side of the street. You have to admit that you might have been wrong, so you have a chance to finally get it right.

Most of all, this requires you to keep going. To keep seeking and searching. To not give up. To realize that the things you most want are not ones you will find but ones you will build. To realize that self-certainty is a product of sincere self-approval. Not the kind where you can brainwash yourself into thinking you're alright with who you are, but the one that is authentic.

There's a small but sharp fear we all feel when it comes to being who we really are, doing what we really want. When we think of stepping outside of the people we've invented so that we might meet the ones we actually are, there's this instant sense that our hearts have taken a small cold-plunge, and we begin to look for ways in which people might poke holes, reveal us to ourselves, remind us that the things that are enough for us very well may be the ones that render us not enough for others.

Authenticity is vulnerability because it splits our lives in two—we are no longer able to chameleon to keep connections above water. We have to face the reality of who has only liked us for the people we pretended to be. We have to accept that even at the fullest, most honest and beautiful expression of who we are, there will be unhealed people who are still playing the games that we used to participate in at the height of our own self-dissatisfaction, and they may want us to engage again, they may want to diminish our lightness, our steadfastness, our happiness, our light in an effort to feel less contrast about the absence of their own.

It is in these moments that we must realize it is our own love, pouring out and cradling around the perimeters of our own life, that can be the only antidote.

True joy is not a mental equation that we arrive at. Things are not beautiful because of their proximity to others. We do not love someone because we have loved another less, we do not marvel at the mountains because we have looked at the hillside and thought, *not enough*. Each of these things stands full within its own essence, and our job is to determine whether we are the ones with the hearts to appreciate them, with the eyes to see them in their entirety. Not everyone will look up at what's magnificent and believe that it is so, but that does not render what they are looking at less extraordinary. It means it is not for them. It is not their inspiration, nor their source. It is not their person to love or path to walk on.

When you come into an assuredness of who you really are, you will find that your own self-satisfaction has a rippling effect on everyone you come across, that you think of. All of a sudden, you wish them the best in the sincerest way. You hope that they all find joy, find healing, find those who will love them completely and who they will love in return. Because the bigness of their lives is no longer something that has the power to shrink your perception of your own, because the scale at which you are seeing things was not developed from believing you are better than someone, but that you are enough, finally, for yourself.

To heal from comparison seems, at the beginning, like you must find a way to supersede what's threatened you, to come out on top again. In reality, it is finally exiting the pageant you didn't realize you entered; understanding that you are not a commodity, you are a living, breathing, feeling organism, with intentions and hopes and dreams and a future. You are unique entirely to yourself, and the only real way to gauge how well you are or are not doing is to have the courage to go inward, and to feel. To truly be honest with yourself, to keep going when you don't feel finished, to let your roots sink deeper when you are in something you want to last. To realize that none of us will ever maintain seamless lives, but we are all capable of having one we are in some way proud of. We are all capable of deciding what is worth our efforts, our energy, our fight.

Because if you are silently competing with the person next to you, you are becoming a version of the person next to you. If you are silently competing with the person you believe has wronged you, you are becoming a version of the person who has wronged you. If you are silently competing with someone you believe to be doing better than you, you are becoming a version of the person you believe is doing better than you.

These things are acting as your muse.

What you create in response becomes an energetic extension, and so your focus must be on the essence of which you'd like to emulate.

Sometimes, the reason why we hyper-fixate on these comparisons is because they act as unconscious motivators. We want to feel a rush of momentum, and if we cannot find it organically, we make ourselves move out of fear or force. What we don't realize is that, too, becomes part of the greater experience, often in ways we grow to not prefer.

When you're pushed, you're moved an inch.

When you're called, you can walk miles.

That is the difference between how we engineer our drive either out of vengeance—a desire to be better—rather than simply and wholly enough. The former runs out of bandwidth, eventually. It never quite gets us to where we really want to be.

Imagine the funeral of a great artist or writer. Would Hemingway's life be summed up as being better than Kerouac, so he was enough?

Of course not.

The entire premise of attempting to be better than someone so as to be rendered enough is false.

What you'd ultimately like to leave as your legacy is a standalone objective. The most lasting and notable thing you do with your life will never be only what happened to you, what hurt you endured, what failures you valleyed through, or what you lost. The most defining qualities of your life will be what you produced, created, nurtured, or became.

Always.

It's crucial that you're mindful not only of who you are keeping near you, even just mentally, but also what. If the people you are competing with are your idols, the things you utilize, touch, or consistently return to in an effort to create are your altars. Your phone screen is your altar. Your desk is your altar. Your text messages are your altar. Your subscriptions are your altar. Your clothing is your altar.

These are your offerings.

These are the things you see most frequently, engage with most frequently.

This is where you create and place essence and sentiment and representation of who and what you want to be. And so more than what you complain about, or feel resistance toward, or even say you want, this is what life accepts and interprets as your requests and prayers to your future self.

It's not a function of magical thinking or superstition, but a simple reality of how the subconscious mind operates. What you associate becomes fused together for you. What you consistently expose yourself to becomes so familiar, it is eventually preferred, defaulted to. What you say most often begins to form elements of your inner narrative, the way in which you dictate who you are and how you will interact with the world.

These things are more foundational than you realize.

So if you find yourself at a place where you feel a constant heaviness produced by the ways in which you imagine you don't measure up, it's not time to change what you're quantifying but to stop measuring altogether. To stop using your evaluation of others as a driving force for your own evolution or a way in which to feel affirmed when everything else within you is quietly saying—*not quite this, not quite yet.* It's a calling to a far greater change, a bigger recalibration. Rather than setting your sights on what's on either side of you, you just begin to look ahead. You take what is unsettled within you and you make peace. You find resolve.

You build a life so big and so good, it renders any competition irrelevant.

Not because it's better or worse than anyone else's, but because in its truth and wholeness, any comparison at all becomes obsolete.

"Don't shrink your life to meet your comfort zone; expand your vision to meet your standard.

READ THIS WHEN YOU WANT TO CHANGE YOUR LIFE BUT YOU DON'T KNOW WHERE TO START

If you would like to change your life, it is already different. The presence of such a desire is the truest sign that something inside your heart has already shifted, something inside your mind has already changed. Now, the journey is about getting your outside experience to reflect the inner one. The breakthrough is not the end, it's the beginning. It is the moment in which you experience a reality so misaligned to what you feel inside, you are forced to stop and look around and start asking questions. It is the first instance in which you recognize that you are more than what your circumstances currently indicate, that you are more than what your past has proven, that you are more than what you are currently feeling. That you are more than you can even fully imagine yourself to currently be.

The rest becomes a matter of practice.

You have to let your new self-image seep into you enough that it begins to inform your lived experience, and that is where most people get stuck—somewhere between bridging the person they sense themselves to be and the current reality that tells a very different story. Somewhere between the discomfort of the new and the discomfort of the old, and which weighs more heavily, which pushes them more firmly, which would be more worth it, what will really matter. It's through this process that most people begin to wonder why you can know, at the deepest level, what they are meant for and who they are meant to be, and yet at the same time keep reaching for the things that will only hold them back from actually becoming those people.

This is the period in which the fire of your vision must burn stronger than that of your discomfort, because you might be uncomfortable.

You will have to not only brave the unknown but build a home there. You will have to face what you had been running from, only to realize that it was not the fear, but the act of avoiding it, that was controlling you most of all. You will have to learn that you become what you let yourself get used to, because what you get used to is what you inevitably come to prefer, and what you prefer is what you most effortlessly return to, and what you most effortlessly return to is what you start to crave, and what you start to crave is what you want to keep doing, and what you keep doing is who you inevitably come to most distinctly be.

The space between where you are and where you want to be will be bridged not by what you do once, but what you do consistently. Those micro-shifts become massive breakthroughs, and past impossibilities become present realities—they are tipping points that are reached incrementally, inch by inch. We don't wake up one day and discover everything to be different, we wake up and realize that we have outgrown our old normal and are now tasked with defying our comfort zones for long enough and often enough to build one that helps us build what we actually want, rather than falling back into what we assume is all that we could ever handle, ever manage, ever create, or ever deserve.

This part of the journey is also where most people revert back to the familiar, and that is when those familiar lives begin to subtly malfunction, gradually coming apart at the seams. They discover, slowly, that they can no longer force what they know is not right, they can no longer engage with what they do not want, they can no longer fake it—not for a moment longer. It's at this point that so many of us misinterpret strength as the ability to continue holding it all together, when in fact, strength is more often the willingness to let it all go. To open your hands, and notice what leaves and what remains. Most frequently, the life that you have been forcing—the life built for a version of you that you no longer are—passes without much effort, and that inner, gnawing sense that you are meant to experience something more inspiring, something more meaningful, something more beautiful, begins to take a deeper and firmer hold.

If you would like to change your life, you can do it in a day. In a moment, in an hour.

If you would like to change your life, all you must do is plant one seed of differentiation, and then let it take root.

Book the flight, look for the job.

Open your calendar and write "moving day" somewhere in the future, and then make that not the aspiration but the plan.

When you want to reach for your vices, remember your values.

If it is impossible to make concrete changes, make softer ones. Take one more breath before you react with negativity. Correct a self-defeating thought. Write down your gratitude as though you had already been the recipient of all that you desire. Go for a walk when you'd normally stay still. Let yourself rest when you'd normally keep moving. Reach out when you'd normally withdraw. Step back where you'd normally overextend.

These small gestures are not small, they are revolutionary.

They begin to draw the new boundaries of your comfort zone.

Once we do something once, it is easier to do it again, and then again.

Not because any one of those things will actually alter the course of your future, but because they have altered the experience of your now—even slightly. They have introduced a new factor into the equation, a new brushstroke on the canvas, a new element into the universe that is you.

The fact of you wanting to change your life is not always the result of your inability to be present, to appreciate, or to accept that there is an aspect within all of us that will constantly want more. The fact of you wanting to change your life, if felt more and more consistently over time, is often the result of some invisible, inner knowing that there is something and someone more…that you are meant to be.

Real change is usually not a sudden breakthrough, but a small gesture of differentiation—us moving in a way that's slightly different than how we had before.

It's found within the tiny glimmers that peer through and reach you, unexpectedly. The small moments where you think of just one more thing you could try. Fate is often stumbled upon. The pieces pull together in ways that are often so quiet, so unassuming, in the heat of your fear, you can look right past them. You may know at the deepest level that you are meant for something more, or different, and yet don't recognize that the journey of a hundred miles is composed of steps—small steps that are insignificant until they are taken consistently.

These little things grow to become something bigger than the sum of their parts. Within your process, you rediscover your confidence, your motivation. The bigger picture begins to cohere itself, and once again, you have something to believe in, to fight for, to hold onto. You realize, slowly but surely, that the fork in the road was a matter of you not knowing how to engage with the life you have found yourself in, and learning to do so is the character development required to be able to immerse yourself in it completely.

If you attempt to seek the greater purpose or impetus that this unlikely moment may be acting as, you will always find it. And you will find it not because it is always easily or inevitably there, but because that is what the human spirit does—it finds, it makes. And while your dead-end might seem like a road in which you were unceremoniously left at the end of, it's more the result of a world that slowly taught you to deny the wiring in your brain that seeks to form connection, that recognizes opportunity and acts. You have only ever been asked to do what you can with what you have, and what you have is exactly what you need, even in the lack, even in the blank spaces.

What is not there or has not been; what has left or has not seemingly come as easily as you imagined it would, is also offering a sort of framing, a contrast, a necessity.

We live as though it's all a given, an endurance game—that life is something that is only to be tolerated. As though we could shield ourselves from the hurt by not taking the risk when the only real risk is not giving it all while we still could. Failing to live on the edge of our hope, our faith. Not doing what we wanted to do while we could still do it. Not loving the people who were in front of us while they were still there. Not being who we had the capacity to be while we were still in the moment.

No longer waiting for the breakthrough, but understanding that it is only a micro-shift that can set off a domino effect within our lives—that the biggest things begin with the smallest ones, and they're all around us, quietly asking us to realize. To see.

The most unlikely moments often contain within them a piece of yourself you have spent a lifetime looking for.

Find it.

Carry it with you toward your next horizon.

•

You don't have to change your entire life overnight. Just do one thing a little better than you did yesterday. Then do it again.

READ THIS WHEN YOU CARE TOO MUCH ABOUT WHAT OTHER PEOPLE THINK

The more you like something, the less you will need other people to. The less you need other people to, the more they will.

Focus on how your life feels rather than how you imagine it looks. That's where your true journey begins.

READ THIS WHEN YOU DON'T FEEL WORTHY OF LOVE

You are worthy of love if you are willing to love.

That's all it takes.

Sometimes it's attraction that draws us into another person, sometimes it's admiration. Sometimes it's circumstance or dumb luck. What crosses our paths at the onset hardly matters as much as what happens afterwards. We often think that if someone is right for us, it will become evident because our paths will begin to run parallel to one another; the lives we had will merge in some fated way, and we will be so clearly and evidently paired.

In reality, when we really love someone, we choose them.

We choose them every day.

Our paths begin to wind and curve in the same directions because we keep showing up to the same places, in the same ways, and loving them there.

Our lives don't join with another person's because they hold us up in their heads and tally up all of our objectively positive and desirable features and traits and attributes. Most of us eventually arrive at a place where we must admit that no matter how brightly some things may sparkle on the surface, if it doesn't click beneath, it doesn't have legs. It doesn't have life.

You grow to love someone each time they are your sounding board. Each time they remember how you take your coffee. Each new experience you have together and each time you reminisce on the ones you've had. You grow to love someone when you are challenged, and choose each other. When you mess everything up and still are forgiven. When you keep showing up, again and again, until your love runs deeper than the eye can see.

That is when people become most beautiful to us.

We tether our hearts to them each time we turn to one another for solace, for friendship, for faith. Over time, these threads either wrap themselves around us and pull us into one; or they're broken, piece by piece. The certainty we find in love is not in the evaluation of how enough we are to be loved, but by how much loving we have done. How much we have given and received.

Are you willing to show up for someone in their hardest hours and then still rise the next day and see them with all of the mystery and attraction and intrigue that you felt at the beginning?

And are you willing to love yourself enough to accept that pouring your love into a person who does not have the container to receive it is a cruelty to yourself, and to the hearts that are ready and waiting?

To love someone completely requires you to become the biggest version of yourself. It requires you to grow, alone and together. It requires you to accept your fault lines as openings that allow you to find each other more deeply; as ways in which you can take what was fractured and heal it back more strongly than it existed before. It requires you to forgive, both them and you, for what you didn't know, for how you reacted before you knew how to respond, for the person you were, for the person you're still working to become. It requires grace.

To love someone completely requires the recognition that love itself is one big light that bears itself down onto your life and shows you to yourself. That everything intensifies with its presence—the good becomes better, the bad becomes more clear. To love someone completely is to realize that love itself is a hollowing out of the ways you've hidden yourself, from the old things that made you feel safe. To love someone completely is to agree to a greater life, and that agreement often comes with you parting ways with your smaller one, even if it was your safe haven, even if it was once the answer to a question previously asked.

Even if it hurts to say goodbye.

We often think of love as a happenstance when it is in fact a calling. It is a heavy question of what we will sacrifice, what we will be vulnerable for, what we will be brave enough to do. We don't stumble upon love, we find someone we most want to be in love with, and then we build. We work to make it so.

Our soulmates are not just our other halves, but in many ways, our silent teachers, our unseen heroes, our invisible healers, the ones who make us better not because they are asking that of us, but because the virtue of their presence generates a renewal of our spirit. Because we are more whole—both for the light we see and the shadows we face—now that they are there.

And that is why we cannot give up on it.

Not because love is a milestone or a way in which we may insulate ourselves from loneliness, but because it makes us more human than we were before.

Because we will one day look back and realize it was the thing most worth doing all along.

Love is not earned. It's experienced. It's when the alive part of you connects to the alive part of someone else, and those parts intertwine and create their own universe together. There are no requirements for entry to this sacred meeting. There is only the willingness to be seen, the willingness to be turned away from the unwilling, and the willingness to keep going until you find the person who transforms your life, forever.

READ THIS WHEN YOU DON'T KNOW WHAT YOU WANT

Can you remember how it felt when you've gotten it right before?

It's not overthought. There's an offhandedness about it. It's a simple yes, not a complicated yes. Not a yes that's arrived at or rationalized to. It's not a yes that is a conclusion, it's a yes that's gentle and firm at first, and then grows as more details are filled, as color is poured in, the framework set, the bigger picture more completely seen.

It always begins with a simple hunch, a gesture.

This would be a good idea.

I should do that.

I've always wanted to live there.

I might want to reconnect with them.

I feel like someone should create this.

I think this is my next right move.

It's never more than that, because at the beginning, your instinctive yes is just a seed.

We imagine that it will be this overwhelming knowing, but often, it's more that experience, consistency, and time compounds upon that small, intuitive "yes," and turns it into a bigger one.

If you cannot recall any strong "yes" that you have experienced in your lifetime, could you recall a smaller, quieter one? Is there an item you love, a person whose presence you enjoy, a place you like to go, a picture you like to look at, an account that makes you smile, a way you take your tea in the morning that feels so right?

Asking yourself the biggest and most important questions of your life is a hard ask for an inner guidance system that already lacks clarity.

Remember that wanting is an integral to human life as breathing, as motion. It's the driving force behind why we reach, why we hold, why we settle, and also why we feel unexplainable uneasiness when we let ourselves plant roots a few inches too deeply into the things we have wound stories around, built belief into, and only convinced ourselves are right when they are not sitting plainly with us at our core.

Wanting is a feeling state—one that is always within us, and if it's become inaccessible, we have to start reconnecting the threads from the simplest ways, first.

Want has been made to seem like something selfish, something childish, something unrealistic, and something we must defy in pursuit of higher and more orderly values.

However, want is actually the electromagnetism that makes our inner compass point north.

We are meant for what we want, because it is an indicator of what we already have but do not recognize, or have not fully materialized into the world outside of us yet still desire to.

Our connection to our gentle, consistent wanting state often gets butchered when we live our lives out of integrity. That's when our signals get caught in the crosshairs. If we are constantly trying to gather reasons to convince ourselves to want something more than we actually want it, we aren't quite stabilizing ourselves or grounding in the way we might think we are. In fact, we are just confusing our inner guidance systems in our attempt to override them.

Those inner guidance systems—unless in the presence or experience of real and immediate danger in which action needs to be taken instantly—are usually not demanding with their information or instruction. The communication is often simpler.

When we try to convince them otherwise, we end up warping the direction of our lives.

There's a deep sense of panic or uneasiness that can come with the recognition that you don't know what you want, but of course, you do. Want is a part of your operating system, always. It's the discernment process you're struggling with, as you'll want a variety of things throughout the course of your life, and in any given experience or time. So it's up to you to choose what you're going to prioritize, value, or energize with your thoughts, focus, or behaviors.

What you are inspired by are the things you are aware you want.

What you are triggered by are the things you are not aware that you want.

Just because you come into a greater and fuller awareness of the breadth and depth of your wanting states does not mean that it is always time to act upon those wants. Sometimes, we resist knowing it because it feels like recognition and action are one in the same, but they aren't.

Sometimes, we can acknowledge what we ultimately want while also honoring what we temporarily need. Sometimes, we just need to rest and recalibrate, allow our bodies to go through a wintering season, allow ourselves to reconnect to our center. Sometimes, we don't know what we don't know. Connecting to our wants is as much about recognizing what lights us up versus what subtly turns us away as much as it is going out into the world and stumbling upon things that give us those same reactions, that we had maybe not considered prior.

Often, the issue isn't that you *don't* know what you want. It's that you *do* know what you want but you need to gather energy to execute, more information to make it increasingly whole and complete, a strategy, a plan, or a fuller vision of what you might do next with your life.

When we are impulsive about acting on our wants, it's because we're trying to escape some other kind of discomfort.

Wanting is not a negative thing, it's a warm and constant knowing that threads your entire life together—one experience at a time.

What we want is not a buried gold we are meant to go out into the world and seek; it's a state of perceptivity that we have to reconnect within ourselves and then apply.

It's already there.

It's around us and in us.

Opportunities, chances, and doorways surround us at all times, too.

Reconnecting with what we want is actually just developing the capacity to see that. We often deny what we organically want when it feels dead-ended, as though acknowledging the impulse would be a pain in and of itself, as there is nowhere to go with it, nothing waiting for us but disappointment.

It's simply untrue.

When we are having the experience of wanting something, what is actually happening is that we have temporarily disconnected from it. In that moment, the loss can feel all-consuming and we adopt this perspective that we are fundamentally without that thing we desire, and our lives are meant to be a journey of finding or building outside of ourselves and then placing ourselves into that reality, so as to render us having, finally.

This never works because the threads of reconnection only exist within the moment. We find ourselves wishing to feel more stable, more successful, more beautiful, more put-together, more loved, and so we attempt to emulate or create second-edition renderings or facsimiles of what we've seen other people who we assume to be experiencing those feelings do in order to have them ourselves.

But if you interviewed the people you found to be the most overflowing and abundant in the characteristics, traits, and qualities that you most desire to have, you would probably find that many of them also feel disconnected from those experiences, no matter how it may seem on the surface.

You are not observing or notating their experience. You are observing and notating your own thread of reconnection with someone else. What you believe them to be doing or having is not always an accurate indicator of how they feel about their own selves. But it is always an accurate indicator of the capacity you have to feel about your own self, that you are trying to find your way back into.

Through the course of your life, you'll meet people who are by worldly measures successful beyond belief, and yet still feel riddled by insecurity, doubt, self-loathing, and fear. Likewise, you'll meet people who have very little accomplished by the world's standards, and yet are rich beyond comprehension in love, family, friendship, fulfillment, and joy. This is because the threads to those things connect inside, first. Then they become a lens through which we are able to see the world. When we are disconnected—which is almost always the product of our focus being disproportionately placed upon the ways in which we *might not* have those things—it's our seeing capacity, our perceptive abilities that are short-ended, not our actual lack of them.

If you want to feel beautiful, you have to find a way to feel beautiful now, just as you are. Not as a surrender to your perceived inadequacy, but in transcendence of it. For one glimmering moment, your ability to reconnect to the sensation of beauty will put the lens of beauty back on you. It will become a color that you are once again able to paint your life with. With continued focus and consistency, you'll be able to move in the direction of expanding beauty—both rooting yourself in a deep knowing and opening yourself to new horizons. This applies to almost every desirable trait or feeling state of life—success, stability, love.

This is the nature of the breakthrough.

Instead of thinking you want to be more successful, begin thinking about what assets you have that you are not taking advantage of currently.

Then you will begin to see success everywhere.

We all dream and fantasize about far-off goals, but almost never realize that the journey to them begins in the car that's in the driveway. We get in there and we start moving.

In some ways, this simplifies and almost neutralizes our wants in a way that some may find less appealing and under-stimulating. When we recognize that the embodiment of what we want is the natural and inevitable end result of a certain pattern of choices, behaviors, and actions—done with an openness to adaptability and growth—the idea of "getting what we want" can seem kind of boring, and we lose interest.

This is another key distinction point. It's where the truly committed are separated out from those enamored by the idea but without a heart in the game.

When you recognize that the journey to having what you want is as humbling as it actually is, it will remove a lot of false wants from your psyche.

You'll begin to realize that you don't actually care about two thirds of the things you think you want or say you want, and they're mostly actually just acting as guides to the real things you want, but fear you cannot have, experience, or be.

Once those are out of the way, you're met with a newfound clarity.

In place of the smaller consolation prizes where you dip down low and feel your emptiness, and survey the depth and severity with which you are disconnected from your truth, to the rapid rise and seeming victory of having it all at once and proving to the world that you do, you begin to exist in a more peaceful equilibrium where you are excited to wake up in the morning and build.

That's the richest, most fertile ground of your entire life.

And it's not easy to get to.

The ways in which your mind will be warped and your attention both thwarted and withheld in the dark corners that do not allow you to weave together threads of connection, possibility, ease, and clarity are overwhelming and everywhere. Your life will be more about identifying these and avoiding them than it will trying to uncover your pockets of inspiration and motivation. Most people are of the belief that disenchantment occurs organically, and it's faith we have to find. In reality, it's love and possibility, organic creativity, and effortless connection with our true selves that springs up from inside of us, at all hours, at all times—it is the barrier of thoughts and perceptions that lead us astray that we have to learn to manage.

A lot of people know how to make money, few know how to have it.

A lot of people can envision their elevator speech, but few know how to operate the day-to-day responsibilities that it would take to build it.

A lot of people know how to stoke romantic or sexual interest, few know how to turn it into a lifelong dance of deep companionship and true love.

This is because we spend the majority of our lives in the arena of wanting, not having. What we practice, constantly, is the act of wanting, and not having. What we master is the state of wanting, and not having. They are two entirely different things.

When we are in the practice of having, we are living in this exploratory state where we are always thinking of how to use what we have to create what we want. In this, we experience an ongoing, colorful, exciting, beautiful fulfillment of desire. It happens in small ways and big ones, every day. Our baseline approach to existence is to *make the best of anything*, whereas when we are in the practice of wanting, our approach is to *desire the best of everything*.

There's an ego block that we have to overcome in order to do this, and it's humility.

If we conceive of the concept for an illustrious business in an entirely new or even somewhat adjacent field to us that we have familiarized ourselves somewhat but now dream of immersing ourselves completely, the first steps to actually making the transition are just making a smaller version of the bigger picture occur in the reality we have now.

This is the arena in which we will receive the lessons we need to learn what we need to know in order to operate at that larger scale and level. It's a two-fold intention, on life's behalf—it's as though our experience is always saying to us: *show me that you can, and then I will let you.*

The way we show is not by visualizing, or intending, or even really speaking about what we are going to do.

The way we show is by doing, often in simple and somewhat humbling ways.

If the moment of humility is not something you are willing to do in order to get to where you claim you want to be, then you probably don't want to be there as much as you think you do. That want is most likely a coverup want for something deeper and more authentic, but that you are too afraid to acknowledge.

Just ask the myriad people who started their businesses in garages, began as understudies and shadows, who apprenticed and practiced in the quietest ways. Where they ended up would seem so grand and overwhelming, it would appear to the outside world as though their lives were a stroke of brilliance and genius and luck. But that's also why their disposition tends to have a more grounded undercurrent. It's because the people who actually have it know what it took to get it. They know the levers that had to be pulled, the people enlisted, the amount of discipline, sacrifice, and consistency that got them there, and they tend to stand at a stark opposition with those whose success stories are more a smoke-and-mirrors than actual substance.

The smoke-and-mirrors success stories are grandiose in their nature. They are quick and occur on timelines. They are rushed and they are oriented toward other people's perceptions. Whereas sincere success often belongs to the person you first overlook or doubt. In their quiet commitment to their own path, there is an openness to their journey. They are willing to do *whatever it takes, for as long as it takes,* to arrive at their desired horizon. The process of getting there is as interesting and compelling to them as having arrived.

It's that level of clarity that you are seeking.

Want is somewhat beaten out of us from a very early age.

We are taught that what we want is a negative. That getting it or even acknowledging it worsens our character and depletes us as human beings.

In reality, it's the people whose needs and wants go dangerously unmet that adapt into the most soulless, uncaring versions of who they might be. Worn down to their own survival instincts, it's people who aren't being seen that are most demanding of attention; it's people who feel unfulfilled that are most critical of those pursuing meaning; it's people who feel the least joy that are most damning of those experiencing it; it's people who feel they're at a place of destitution that more easily justify unethical ways of balancing their own scales.

It's when we don't know how to pursue what we want without conscious consideration of others that we become what others would perceive as greedy.

But even greed is actually a signifier of an internal emptiness, a void that cannot be filled, because outside accumulation didn't create it. It's usually an indicator of a way in which other, more fundamental and desired wants are not being met.

Most of us exist with the unconscious belief that if we get what we want, we will become monstrous, insatiable versions of ourselves, as though satisfying our true desires and needs is a way of fueling and aggravating our worst qualities, traits, and behaviors.

The reality is that confidence is built from getting what we want.

Pursuing what we want.

Becoming what we want.

Our ability to build, cooperate, learn, grow, develop, open up, love, expand, think, and change is all contingent upon us knowing what we want or the feeling as though we can get what we want.

And in that sense, it's crucial to remember that the peacefulness and stability in your life almost always has its center in your innermost call being answered.

Another misbelief is that we take advantage of what we get used to; that if we lack awareness of how much we have already received, we will once again become single-mindedly determined to accumulate more and more, never truly knowing what it is to be fulfilled, not thinking about others, and simply living our lives as though our only goal is to acquire, accumulate, and impress.

The truth is that our wants are supposed to evolve as our journey moves forward.

We did not come here to spend every season in passiveness; we came to do something fulfilling and beautiful and true.

In many ways, the purpose that you're most seeking for your life, that sense of true meaning and complete fulfillment, has its origins in want. Just as wanting is a living, moving thing—it evolves as we do—our relationship to it often determines how well and easily we are able to move through the journey of our lives.

You are meant for what you want at the deepest level of yourself.

Your denial of these spaces and these instincts and pure knowing is what is holding you back from seeing and acting upon it completely.

Buried beneath what we imagine we want on the surface exists the deeper wells that are asking to be filled, and it's through the experience of contrast—first knowing what it is to live *without* that want fulfilled—that we become most completely able to actualize it.

We all get what we want, one way or another. It's just how cognizant we are of that want and whether or not we find healthy and sustainable ways to pursue it that really makes the difference. A lot of the time, our most self-sabotaging behaviors are actually a function of us *getting exactly what we want* but not realizing the unconscious benefit or function of what it is we're seeking. A lot of the time, when we don't know how to plainly state or claim what we want, we have a way of turning it into something we need. Where we could have made the path clean, we dirty it; we create tension and contrast, imagining that the only way we can actually receive what it is we desire is if there is some necessity for it.

There is a different way to approach the future.

Rather than fighting our inherent sense of wanting, telling ourselves we can have a little bit of it, or that close enough is good enough, or that we don't *actually need it* so as to render our pursuit of it irrelevant or unimportant, we can sit in quiet acceptance of the purity of want.

Human beings want connection.

We want love, we want safety, we want wellness.

We want self-actualization, purpose, happiness, meaning, and hope.

And though there are so many things we might use to gloss over those wants, so many status symbols and milestones and representations of desires fulfilled, it is only within our hearts that we know the truth. It is only within our bodies that we can sense whether or not we have hit the nail on the head, whether we are in the arena we so care to be, whether we are living a life that is true to us, a life we would be proud of at the very end of it all.

And the greatest courage, the most undeniable resilience of character, comes in the moment when we decide we will let go of what is not ours—no matter how it may seem on the surface, no matter how many people may believe we are making a mistake, no matter how little it would make sense to them, no matter how much we'd be judged or condemned for it—and watch as life almost effortlessly rewards us with the gift of what *is* ours.

That's the thing about wanting—it's not something we have to always consciously identify and then actively pursue. Sometimes, just removing the impulse to sabotage or eschew our wanting state is enough for life to become responsive to it and start showing us ways to make it reality. Sometimes, what we really have to reconcile is the false idea that we are not enough, not worthy, for the lives that are already ours or are about to be. Sometimes, we have to let go of the old patternings that tell us if life is not imbued with suffering and denial, it is not noble or realistic. Sometimes, we have to admit that we've been talking ourselves into wanting something when the very center of our beings is communicating otherwise.

And sometimes, we have to have the grit to be able to acknowledge that the want has been there all along. If we were to trace the threads back to their origins, we'd find a lot of them stemming from our earliest days, our genesis experiences, the first instances where we got a glimpse of who we are and who we'd like to be.

Back then, our knowledge of ourselves was so simple, though the ways in which we thought that it might be expressed were likely limited, too.

We knew if we wanted to compete, perform, or teach.

We knew if we wanted to be seen, known.

We knew if we wanted to see our friends, create, make art, explore.

Returning to a healthy relationship with our wanting state is often simplifying things back to the way they once were, the way we once knew them.

Beneath the wanting that can come across as too precise, too pointed, too tense, is often a deeper ache that's been ignored, for too long.

Beneath some people's desire for recognition of their work exists a desire for validation. Beneath other people's is just a desire to prove something to their own selves. Beneath some people's desire to dress well or look good is a desire to be included. Beneath other people's is a desire to embrace their love of style as an artform. Beneath some people's desire to date many people is the desire to be completely known, and accepted, and chosen, safely, by one. Beneath other people's is a desire to expand their horizons and explore potential connections. Beneath some people's desire to excel is a desire to root. Beneath other people's is a desire to rebuild their lives entirely. Beneath some people's desire to blame is a desire to thwart responsibility, to remain unchanged. Beneath other people's is a desire to organize responsibility and stop over-claiming what isn't theirs. Beneath some people's desire to confront is a desire to be shown they are cared enough for to fight with. Beneath other people's is an inability to regulate impulsive emotions. Beneath some people's desire to create is a desire to have their livelihood, their human experience, documented in a way that would outlive them, that would serve something greater than their momentary itch to make something beautiful and real. Beneath other people's is no such long-term goal, just the genuine and momentary sense that there's something worth making, here and now.

We can't always measure or gauge what someone else is wanting or where they are coming from.

All we can accept is that human behavior often has motivation, and at the root of human need is myriad things, ranging from belonging to becoming. And that if what we want feels out of reach or we feel as though we are at odds with it, always pursuing but never being met or fulfilled, it's usually because beneath the surface-level want exists a more honest desire, one that it's in our best interest to uncover and embrace.

What we want is integral to who we are, but that does not mean life is meant to be a series of simply identifying wants and then receiving them, seamlessly and without growth or further effort, and that whenever our wants are not being instantaneously met, we are somehow off-path or mistaken or lost.

There are also times during which we are meant to not know.

There are also times during which we are meant to want for something bigger than what we could create or receive in one fell swoop.

There are also times during which we are meant to sort of know but test our faith.

There are also times during which we are meant to just explore, discover, find deeper layers of ourselves, exist in the not-knowing, and see what sprouts from there.

It's often in those very same periods where we are most unsure of where we are going next that we glean the most information and clarity about ourselves that eventually allows us to move forward and find the next big thing our lives will be devoted to.

There isn't just merit in the waiting, in the unknown—there's also infinite possibility.

Without periods of rest, of open-mindedness, of willingness, and of growth, we would exist forever on a compulsive pattern of wanting what it is we've always wanted, finding our way to it, letting it go, again and again, for all of our lives. It's in those introductory periods when we meet people who show us new ways of living or being, we stumble upon our new greatest inspiration, we reconcile the fact that we're ready to shed old layers, or even just acknowledge what is not working, we are actually opening ourselves to new degrees and complexities of want and enabling ourselves to advance in bigger ways.

Part of mastering our wanting state is recognizing that it is the *people we become on the journey to the milestone* that offers far more weight, importance, and meaning than the actual act of arriving there.

Sometimes, recognizing our deepest wants is not a matter of being able to line-item what we desire to create more of in this chapter or season of our existence, but recognizing the lifelong dance we care to partake in, one where we come to know layers and versions of love, of ourselves, of growth, of beauty, of care.

Want is a quiet impulse, and it only exists in the moment. The mind cannot decipher want the way embodied intuition can. Determine how you'd actually like to spend your today. Every other answer will be found in that same knowing space.

READ THIS WHEN YOU'RE ALWAYS WAITING FOR SOMETHING BAD TO HAPPEN

One of the things that most limits our capacity in life is the belief that any measure or degree of success or progress is akin to a house of cards, something that becomes more vulnerable as it grows. In reality, true success is more like adding legs beneath a table.

The more you grow, the more stable you become. The journey should not ever be one where you feel as though you are waiting for the other shoe to drop, as though you're holding your breath until it all falls apart or goes wrong; as though goodness has a limitation, as though life will always balance what is good by what would negate it.

The stronger you get, the stronger you are.

The more you learn, the better you become.

The more you build, the more you have.

The more you become, the more your life expands.

Every step sets you a little more free.

When you think in the sense that the magnitude of goodness must always be balanced out by an equal measure of its opposite, you misunderstand what it means to create truth, what it means to live within your actual power.

Of course, challenges are inevitable to the course, but they aren't meant to uproot you entirely, they aren't meant to be finalities or dead-end signs. If they are? It's usually because what we're being awakened from is something unsustainable, unhelpful, unsupportive to our greater or more complete mission or purpose or truth.

If you think of life like a balancing game in which things must always level themselves out, then you will always remain right where you are.

You will never really change.

If you fear greater degrees of success or growth under the assumption that they must inevitably bring with them greater degrees of pain or duress, you are falling into the trap of the limited thinking that's been keeping you where you are this entire time.

The whole point of growth is that you are more stable than you would have been before.

When things get better, they get better.

And so do you.

Anticipating what could go wrong does not shield you from it; it weakens your defenses. It is the virtue of building a whole life outside of your fear that shields you from the possibility of loss, of hurt. The more coherent you are, the more naturally protected you become.

READ THIS WHEN YOU NEED TO LET GO THOUGH IT HURTS TO DO SO

Do not force it.

Do not force yourself to feel neutrality if you are not neutral yet. You do not force yourself to feel happiness if you are not happy yet.

Let yourself grieve for as long as you need to and do not bottle it up.

Do not make apologies for it.

Do not try to cover or conceal what has impacted you, what has shaken you, what has left scars.

Process, because through that processing, you will learn.

You will learn that you can withstand more than you ever thought. You will learn that you can endure more than you imagine. You will learn that a feeling won't kill you, but the life you bury beneath it because you are afraid to feel it—that might, at the end of the day.

You will realize that it's better to be hurt and to live, than to exist in a state of numbness forever.

If it's not time to let go, it means there's something left to be learned. Something to be reflected upon, gathered, and carried forward. Extract the lesson and lean into it. Study it. The more you ground your newfound knowing into the life you're building on the other side of loss, the more effortlessly the loss will fade with the hours until, eventually, it leaves entirely—almost without you realizing that it did.

READ THIS WHEN YOU FEEL COMPLETELY LOST IN LIFE

All the pieces of your story that have not made sense, that have left you with more questions than answers, that felt like false starts and endless cycles, will eventually reveal themselves to you as perfectly sequenced, perfectly timed, perfectly destined to set you up for all that you would one day come to know and be.

Sometimes, you don't know because you can't know. The virtue of you knowing where it all ultimately leads would short-circuit the process, and the process? It's a regathering. It's where you wake up the parts of yourself that had been laying dormant as potential, where you recover the parts of yourself that you lost to the past, to grief, to fear; where you begin to uncover who you really are and what you really want to be. Your path has taken you to the exact people, places, and experiences that can give you that knowledge. The losses were lessons, written by your own subconscious mind, with the intention of bringing you to your edges and allowing you to see past the walls you had been quietly living inside.

The life you are meant for is the life you actually want. Not the life you are settling for because it feels easiest, because you want to feel safe more than you want to actually experience this world while you are still in it. Not the life that makes your ego feel as though it can compete, but the one that makes your soul recognize that there was never a competition in the first place. The only measure is how fulfilled we are, how much we can appreciate the day we have, the opportunities we're being given, those who have chosen to walk alongside us—all we have, all we are, and all we will one day be.

It is in our highest interest to listen to the discomfort, as it is attempting to lead us to peace. To honor what is not working so we may keep reaching toward what will. To remember that if something is not bringing us wholeness, it is trying to bring us to the piece of ourselves we first must self-realize in order to heal, in order to truly and completely be.

Feeling lost is often a good indicator that you're actually on your own path. If you're too sure of what's next, you're probably following someone else's.

READ THIS WHEN YOU FEEL ALONE AND DON'T UNDERSTAND WHY

Maybe right now, you're alone because whatever you need to learn about yourself can only be learned in solitude. Maybe right now, the pieces of yourself you're finding are fusing a truer self into form, a kind of self that will become a more clear and recognizable match for the places and people and opportunities that are meant to come your way.

Maybe right now, you don't feel good enough because you're going to bring someone to the places where you feel the most unworthy and let them love you there. Maybe right now, it's quiet because you're learning to hear the sound of your own voice. Maybe right now, you feel stuck because you have tried to force stillness when what you really need is to keep going. Maybe right now, you feel lost because you're getting a chance to choose something greater than what you once assumed the best could be.

Maybe right now, you're learning to see yourself with kinder eyes. To give yourself the benefit of the doubt. Maybe right now, you're realizing the value in recognizing how far you've come and allowing that to fuel you forward. Maybe right now, you're giving yourself more credit. Maybe you're giving yourself a second chance. Maybe you're learning how to be with yourself in the quiet hours, the times when you'd rather fill the void with another person's company. Maybe you're learning how to enjoy your own presence.

And maybe right now, life isn't letting you settle somewhere you aren't meant to be. Maybe life isn't allowing you to source comfort somewhere it does not want you to relax into, or get used to, or continue sustaining.

Maybe life is moving you in a different direction.

Maybe life is trying to show you how taking care of the person you are informs the one you will become. Maybe things are happening just as they need to, even if you don't understand their sequence, or order, or reason. Maybe all you're meant to do is take it one day or even an hour at a time. To greet the moment and ask what you should do with it, even if what you should do is sometimes the bare minimum and sometimes revolutionary. Maybe this is the time when you make space for all of those pieces of you to come together, to settle in and find home. Maybe in the midst of the uncertainty, this is life's way of making sure you make peace with yourself.

No matter how alone you may think you are, your aloneness is not the only thing you will ever feel, and it is not the only thing that you will ever be.

No matter what has cracked your heart, no matter what has left splinters of itself inside your psyche, no matter what you have endured or might be enduring, remember that pain has its greatest power when we allow it to completely eclipse our rationale. When it is able to convince us not only of its potency, but its perceived permanence. That it is the only thing that we will ever experience or have ever felt. In the peak of a strong emotion, our minds begin to wind themselves all through our history and project it all out into the future. Seeking, hunting, for proof that we are doomed.

Time and time again, we find what we are looking for.

It is in these moments that you must remember that it is okay to feel the bigness of a feeling that has weight, has impact, has a reverberating effect through your soul. But you do not have to allow it to become the sole, defining element of your personality, your life. You are allowed to hurt and still know you will laugh again, you will smile, you will find good things, and they will find you. Not because you are special or deserve a miracle—though of course you very much do—but because this is the inevitable nature of life. Things come back around, eventually. The sun always rises. The storm always passes. It cannot always be night.

Let hope find you in the unlikely hours. The hours when you have forgotten that what you appreciate about your life has not disappeared, it has temporarily become hidden. Let the storm move through you, because after it is finished?

You will know that truth most completely.

You will see, with fresh eyes, all that was there the entire time.

The waiting periods of our lives—the times when we are still bridging the space between where we have been and where we are going—are as much a part of our stories as anything else. They offer us something potent, something we cannot claim elsewhere. They are our chance to let go of what's not coming with us as we move forward, process what's been left as debris, and decide how we are going to move into our next chapter. The desire to rush past it all is understandable but also an oversight. Because in doing so, we also miss the most important opportunity of all.

Most people think their biggest fear is being alone, but it's also in our alone hours that the most radical shifts and leaps of growth are made. It begs you to consider—do you fear being alone or do you fear no longer being distracted?

Not from your pain, but from your potential.

The true work.

If we are to think of life as a game, then a key element is knowing when to play and when not to.

You aren't needed on the board all of the time.

What we celebrate in public is what we have perfected in private.

It's how we move in our off-hours that determine the nature and efficacy of the ones when we are on. It's also our ability to discern when we are needed or wanted that will diffuse so much tension, pressure and unnecessary work from our lives.

If you think about the way people used to experience one another—and furthermore, each other's work—decades or even centuries ago, you would recognize that there's an element of constant connection that doesn't quite work in our favor. Back in the day, if you left town and started over somewhere new, you were truly gone. You wouldn't be informed of what others were doing unless you called and checked in or went back to visit. Similarly, others wouldn't be getting a streamed play-by-play of your new life in real-time. Today, we leave with an announcement that is seen often not only by those we know are following, but also many we don't even realize are keeping tabs, with positive intentions or not.

Back in the day, people spent longer and longer stretches of time working on something before it was deemed ready to be shared. Back in the day, when you were ready for rest or recluse, you were actually able to take it without a constant stream of emails, thoughts, posts, and other inputs flooding your brain simultaneously.

This is not to say that life in the digital age is without its perks—certainly most of us would take them despite the downsides—but it is to say that it's in our interest to be mindful of the fact that it's not only unnatural for us to be able to watch the lives of everyone we've known from virtually every era of our lives unfold, but that the unconscious knowing that the same is happening to us has a unique way of hindering our growth and our willingness to experiment, shed, adopt new and more authentic concepts of ourselves, or grow in the ways we'd really like.

That's why understanding the importance of your quiet hours is so crucial.

Everything happens in those hours. Everything. As far as you should be concerned, anything happening in the public arena is a ceremonial trophying. All battles are won in the preparation period, and then you bear witness to what has happened in the preparation period once everyone is out on the field. When you sit in awe of a striking performance, or absorb a particularly poignant piece of artwork, or admire someone who has clearly done a lot of personal growth and made progress with themselves, you're never really witnessing a single stroke of genius or talent that exists in a vacuum. You're witnessing countless, tireless hours of effort, of processing, of coming-to-terms, of adapting. You're witnessing the tail-end of a long journey of true devotion.

When we aspire to great things within our own lives, it's often those crowning moments that inspire us most. It's those moments that move us, and compel us, and make us reach for them. What we often underestimate is the fact that those moments were preceded by incredible amounts of private dedication, often more than the average person is willing to offer.

In 2005, the artist Lawrence Weiner created a conceptual mural on a wall in Minneapolis, in which he simply affixed text that read: "Bits and pieces, put together, to present a semblance of a whole."

That sentiment seems to describe the undercurrent of the way we imagine human life to unfold today. Through a combination of both a spotlighting complex, where we see our lives as fodder for content that has to follow a clean and linear storyline and narrative, as well as the impression that if we are not consistent in pinpointing our milestones and progress markers we've ceased to have meaningful lives altogether, we have somewhat convinced our brains to believe that a successful life is a seamless one. That we are not only meant to conform, but that the notable moments cohere together in the stream of our awareness that we think we are meant to be constantly peaking, constantly summering, constantly flourishing.

This tightening of our perception limits our capacity for true human development and life.

What we deny ourselves when we do not have the space to truly rest, to truly relax, to truly allow ourselves to be lost, to not know, and to just exist within those in-between spaces is the chance to actually choose a new path. We deny ourselves development, growth. We deny ourselves the savoring, the embracing of the moment as it is. But more than anything, we deny ourselves the chance to release.

It's the times in your life where it feels as though life is leveling out and you're losing, losing, losing is usually the exact same inflection point at which you're being reborn into the next dimension of yourself. It's natural to both gain and then to grow, to put things to rest, to find closure, to move on.

When we live with the perception that our lives have to follow only the cleanest narratives or that we have to place our stake in the ground at any given point, we are truly capping our ability to change course, to change our minds, to change our lives as a whole.

If life offers you a period of quiet, of alone, of uncertainty, of time when you don't know what's next or you're still establishing yourself in an entirely new arena, or city, or identity—say thank you.

Use it.

Use every single second you are offered.

You will one day look back on those times as the exact same times that the most profound and striking growth of all was occurring. You will also see, clearly, that not every hour of your life is meant to be the crescendo. Not everything is a peak period, and that's not because there's anything wrong with you or that you don't have the capacity for consistency or that you have failed. That is simply because you are honoring the organic tides and motions of what it is to be alive.

In your quiet hours, you are getting a chance to reform yourself—often beyond anything you'd be able to mold or shape during those times when you are most connected and rooted into life.

No longer pinned and anchored to the elements of identity that other people are consciously and unconsciously holding you to, those quiet hours are offering you an opportunity to independently decide who you want to be and then to practice being them.

Our lives were never meant to flow in a succession of victories, wins, and highs, no matter how other people's metaphorical highlight reels have made it seem to be. We ebb and we flow. We go inward and then take it outward. We draw a labyrinth in the sand and then the ocean washes it away. We write one story and find its ending, and begin another where the conclusion used to be.

We learn.

Through the learning, we carry with us tools—which are really just various lenses of awareness; it's the ability to see and re-interpret what we are seeing that changes how we move through the days of our lives.

Absence creates value.

Rarity is actually what makes something more desirable and appreciated.

When we are over-saturating people with ourselves, it's like overwatering a plant.

It dies from over-caring.

In the same way that you cannot plant a seed and then continually dig it up to check on whether or not it's taken root or is beginning to grow, periods of quiet, rest, and hibernation are also required for our personal growth.

Another reason we avoid the quiet hours of our lives is because within them lingers uncomfortable truth–feelings that we carry subtly within us, with no clear outlet or resolve.

When we are undistracted and in a true rest state, we are really left to reconcile with these emotions, which, while uncomfortable, is like performing mental hygiene.

There are many ways in which we attempt to process emotions that end up circumventing them, where we imagine that we are placing our finger on the nose but we are, in fact, distracting ourselves with narrative that seems to release the pressure valve temporarily, but in actuality, keeps us returning to the same or even more heightened feeling states.

There is importance to reflection, to self-understanding.

There is a time to glean wisdom from what we have experienced and to take it with us.

But there are also a large number of emotions that simply want to be felt. Not placed, not psychoanalyzed, not dissected, not hyper-fixated upon.

Just felt.

The capacity to just sit and feel may seem so simple it would elude most of us, but can feel in that moment like a Herculean feat.

That is because in the practice of just sitting and *feeling what we feel*, it can seem as though we are facing a dead end. When we are in the moment with the feeling and have not crafted any kind of reason or meaning for it, it can seem as though it will go on forever. What is most important to remember in these moments is that these feelings, once felt, will release themselves with time, and if they do not, we can then work on building a narrative that allows us to more safely release them with time.

Either way, the groundwork is allowing ourselves to feel.

And that can only happen when we are no longer distracted.

Allowing ourselves to just feel, process, and let go of our emotions—even if we just create a few moments of space each day to focus on our bodies and recognize what is happening within them—can help us clear and sort so much.

The quiet hours often coincide with transition times. Periods where we are not here, nor quite there yet. That, too, offers a gift in itself.

If life is a staircase that we are always climbing, there are points at which we are meant to sit down on a step and rest. When we are meant to laugh, gather, and enjoy. Some steps are lonelier than others. There are a few people who will walk with us from the beginning to the very end. Some will be there for a few steps, but then not others. There is not ever a point when we are excused or released from the staircase of life. We are always walking. This is not to say that we are meant to be in a constant state of growing, accumulating, and scaling—just to say that we begin at one point and end at another. We are always moving, no matter how still we have convinced ourselves we might be.

When we think of planting roots, we somewhat imagine stepping off the staircase and building a home on the sidelines.

In reality, planting roots is a way we learn to carry ourselves.

We are always walking on the path of life.

When we feel stable and sure, it's because we have decided upon a particular stride, and stuck with it long enough that we become not only quite good at it, but it begins to feel second-natured.

The way we feel at home and grounded is by the way we show up to our lives every single day.

It is within the quiet periods—when nobody is walking alongside us or few people are—that we are truly given the opportunity to practice or attempt new ways of being.

While there's also a sense that we need to strike when the iron is hot in life—that we should make the most of our youth, our health, our opportunity—what's also true is that by learning how to carry yourself, you learn how to heat your own irons. You don't wait, or rely, or expect your external circumstances to be the indicators of when you're moving forward versus when you're not, but that you gauge your own journey internally.

Rather than following the patterning of those before you, you dare to move at your own pace and with your own discernment.

The results of which are often more uniquely beautiful and true than you could have conceived.

Though we may turn our roads to walk most closely with those who are tied deeply to our hearts, though we may intersect and collide and learn from others over the years, and though we may only ever know a few instances of complete, physical aloneness in our lifetimes, the truth is that our inner worlds are a place where there is only a voice of one. It is that voice narrating everything, and the essence of that narration dictates our experience. The level of its awareness determines not what we see but how we see it. When we take time to adjust the way we perceive from that level, we actually change the moment we meet. We adjust what options we see, what we can create, what we are able to do.

The idea that you might take your quiet hours to work on that self is not a throwaway option or a consolation prize for not being able to participate in external love the way you might want. It's a lesson on ground zero of what it is to be human. You will wake up with yourself every day and put yourself to sleep every night. You will be left with yourself when everyone around you goes to work and to school and grows up and moves on and once again, it is you and you. You will guide yourself through every heartache, every loss. You will also get to cherish every victory, every success, every resounding win. You are the undercurrent of your entire life experience, the most common denominator.

The arena in which you have full and total control is that of yourself. You cannot control every passing thought or feeling that arises or experience that happens around you or to you, but you decide what you do, regardless of how you feel or have been made to feel. And so that place becomes the most critical, the most potentially world-altering. It's the only thing you can actually, fully assert your will upon and over, and so it is funny to consider that it's the very same place that most people avoid. We spend eternity gazing outward and identifying all that's wrong, but nothing too much changes, because there is little relief in realizing—perhaps my purpose is something far more difficult.

Perhaps my offering must begin with me.

Aloneness is the experience people most fear, and yet it's also the same realm where the most profound and life-altering work can occur. That is likely not a coincidence.

READ THIS WHEN YOU DON'T KNOW WHAT YOUR PURPOSE IS

Instead of thinking of purpose as a fully mapped, invisible route your life is meant to take—and your adherence to it both something you must decode from nothingness and follow without wavering—think of it like little bells that ring when life is asking for volunteers.

Will someone love this person?

Will someone care for that place?

Will someone write that piece?

Can someone sing that song?

The bells are ringing in every moment, of every hour, everywhere. The ones we can hear are the ones we are equipped to respond to. If we say yes, we are then met with a question.

Will we be the one to love someone lost in the most imperfect, human aspects of themselves? Will we be the one to surrender to the quiet long enough to hear the sound, to see the vision? Will we be the one to muster the tenacity and dedication to form a viable idea into a tangible reality that others can experience and feel?

As frequently as purpose is a way in which we are asked to make an intervention—to create something new for the world—the bells are most often trying to bring our attention to a calling within. We are most frequently asked to disrupt an internal pattern, alchemize a feeling, course-correct a generational compulsion, see a silver, shimmering lining of truth beyond the one thought form that acts as a piece of a deeply woven, unconscious narrative that we have built, adopted, and abided by—unquestioningly—over time.

The bells ask us to stop abiding.

In the moment that we realize we are in the heat of a heightened or exaggerated or tail-spinning-out-of-control emotion, we are also in an incomparable, vastly opportune space to dig deeply into the illusion until we arrive at the ground level, the false belief upon which all the rest of the tornado whipped its way around.

Once we are there, we can reconstruct a new experience with a greater truth at the center. What we experience on the outside as an undoing is often an internal signal of an unraveling that will make its way to a revealing. What we find at the end of all the tiny ego deaths we experience when things do not formulate precisely the way we imagine they will is an unwavering truth at the center. *The invisible summer,* as Albert Camus would call it. The part of ourselves that is unmoving, infinite, and waiting for us to return.

Purpose never stops knocking at the door. But if the other noise of life has been made louder, you have likely avoided, missed, and bypassed the callings, again and again. Many of us, at some point or another, find ourselves lost within the leftover shards of the plan for your life you had made when you did not yet know how to listen to the directions from within.

Those dead-end lives are very often made from the desire to reach for the outward callings of purpose that are most visible and most applauded, but these outward callings become available to us once we have been willing and able, to respond to the inward ones. The way we do the little things becomes the way we do the big things. It's what we first master in private that we are applauded for in public. But we can't skip the first part. The first part is the crux of the story.

When we are searching for a purpose, we are often looking for a way to save the world. Purpose is first asking us to save ourselves. To recognize that the only life we are *truly* able to completely control from beginning to end is our own. The only real way to influence other people's behavior is to lead, inspire, and guide—not force, shame, or cajole. It is through understanding our own inner systems that we are better able to understand the world. It is through becoming who we are meant to be that we unlock our capacity for our greatest impact.

If we are each fractal piece of a whole, witnessing and experiencing itself from every different angle, then we would have to acknowledge that the only way to shift the collective is to shift each piece, one by one. We would have to acknowledge that the only piece we are actually able to move is our own. Then we would realize that if we make our own lives an offering to the world we'd rather see, we have already made it fundamentally, unwaveringly, unalterably, permanently, eternally changed.

Your great calling is not a thing that you do, it's a person you become—and then it is the way that person does everything that changes the world.

The points of entry to this journey are so quiet, they are most often completely missed. If we think that purpose is going to arrive at our doorstep one day like a hero's mission, like a job we apply for, a role we are casted in, a clear-cut, life-long, certain knowing that it is this one, sole thing we are here to do—we will wait forever, distracting ourselves with vices, while the doorways to deep meaning open and close in front of our eyes.

Our first assignment is ourselves.

Our first arena is our own lives.

Our first mission is to bring ourselves to our own stable and secure grounding.

The path to following your great calling is not so much about inventing or constructing a self that you think is ideal. It is not the way you think you are seen by the world, but the way *you see the world*. Your great calling is not about figuring out how the door of joy will open. It is realizing you are the door. You are the open. You are the joy.

The experience you are having is you.

The aperture through which you are fielding your life is your 'self.'

Your purpose is not about trying to replace your true self with a grander, bolder, more lovable one, but to realize that your true self is love itself. That it is, inherently, the grandest and boldest and most perfect thing. And when that true self first got bruised, first felt embarrassed, first thought it had to go into hiding—it began to play the game of that which hurt it in the first place. When the truth of who you are was confronted by the closed-off, illusion-self that someone else was holding as a shield, your response became to armor up with a mirroring, parallel one. In truth, the person who first made you feel like you were not enough just needed to be told—*do you know how enough you are?*

When people want to play the game, the way to break through the invitation to re-engage in the illusion is to cut to their own truth inside. It takes a big character not to stoop to the level of the insult but to pierce through it with a thread of light.

Will you, devoting yourself to your own life, change the axis upon which the world turns, end human suffering, and heal people en masse? Probably not, but then again, maybe. You don't know.

Imagine a world of people who are isolated, lost, unhappy, disengaged, uncreative, and lost in their own thoughts. Then consider a world of people who are creating moving art, writing your favorite songs, opening businesses and restaurants and storefronts you would like to frequent, showing one another compassion, living boldly and fearlessly, expressing themselves with fierce authenticity, gathering, connecting, and exploring all that life may be. Most of us would prefer the latter vision, but then don't take it upon ourselves to become one of those people first.

●

Your purpose is not a thing you do, it's a person you become—and it's the way that person does everything that informs what your legacy will be.

READ THIS WHEN YOU AREN'T SURE YOU'LL FIND WHAT'S MEANT FOR YOU

The doors that are right for you will gently open—and you will not have to push or force them. Because the things that are behind them want you and need you as much as you want and need them.

What's meant for you is not something you have to earn or come to deserve. It's a mutual grace; it extends in both directions. What's meant for you is waiting for you as much as you are waiting for it.

READ THIS WHEN YOU FEEL MISUNDERSTOOD

In a world where most people settle, happiness is a foreign thing.

People can understand milestones more than they do meaning. They understand following the course over trailblazing toward your soul. They understand the love that looks right over the one that feels right. They understand what it is to pull your hope by the root and plant sense in its place. They understand a plan that is followed, rather than a life that is engineered; one that is dreamt and built.

Because when you are following your heart, you are going to spend a lot of time in the unknown. You're not always going to see what's next because you're working with an open-ended resource. You're not always going to be able to move in a linear trajectory, because some things have to be revisited, revised, picked back up, and carried forward. Some things pique your interest and within them, a piece of your future is formed. When you are following your heart, you understand that you don't always know what you don't know. You're not working just with the world you can see, but the one you might imagine.

And so if you are in a place right now where you are convinced that nothing is going to work out, this is your sign that you will find everything you fear you won't. That you will have love, have work, have home, have purpose, even if right now it feels as though more is coming apart than coming together.

Because right now, the storm that's formed did not arrive to obstruct your path but to clear your vision. Right now, you are getting a chance to choose from your heart and not your head. You are getting a chance to pick what's real to you over what's real to others. You are getting a chance to defy what you thought life would be and enter an entirely new realm instead.

●

Living within the realm of truth will seem foreign to those on a tightly structured trajectory, one given to them by the world but disconnected from their center. Don't look to insanity to gauge your own clarity. Your own inner knowing will light the way.

READ THIS WHEN YOU'RE PARALYZED BY FEAR

Fearfulness is like an iron shield that our hearts wrap around anything that matters. When we have conflated the feeling of fear with an indication to not proceed, we allow fear to control us, to stop us, rather than to just tell us that we are moving toward something that truly matters. We cannot only avoid what we are scared of; we also end up avoiding everything we actually desire, everything we actually came here to be.

If we do this for long enough, what exists on the other side of the fear begins to feel like an impossible destination. We assume we will just never arrive. We become so used to living in a way where we are numbed out, distracted, always running and making excuses for ourselves, we forget that there is another way. The web of our own justification winds itself so tightly over every corner of our lives, it begins to feel as though we will never be able to break free.

The fortunate thing is that truth is a torch that lights the web on fire with even just the smallest spark. When we act and speak from the place of our deepest and most honest and most sincere and most unwavering true north, everything else begins to fade away in its presence. Like light that bleeds into a dark room when the door is cracked open, the presence of what's real changes everything, all at once, immediately and forever.

What if this pause is not an opportunity to strengthen your will but loosen your defenses? What if you untied your idea of incapability from your unwillingness? What if you let the hesitation soften you into greater openness, rather than harden you into more forceful attachment? What if the idea of deservingness is in itself a limiting concept that could only ever hold you back? What if your only job from here is to open your hands and watch what arrives, and honor what stays?

When we engage in fear, we make an agreement with the fear to feed it and keep it alive. It cannot exist without our input, our mental entertainment, our permission, our allowance, our engagement.

Because it is not conscious.

So it requires our consciousness to stay alive.

When we choose not to interact with it, when we withdraw the offering of our attention—even if the fear pulls at our nervous systems, asking us to re-engage—we begin to find that it weakens.

Fear controls us when we invest more into the problem than the solution. Fear is a compulsive state in which we are stuck from motion, from action, thinking moving forward will hurt worse. That's part of the illusion. It keeps us stuck by thinking that the river of life is what causes us pain. That by confronting the grief, cleaning up our side of the street, we will somehow engender ourselves to greater suffering than what we are experiencing now.

But it simply isn't true.

The river isn't the pain source, it's our disengagement from life—from living—that is.

Life is not terrifying, it's the idea that a bruise or a wound could inspire us to withhold ourselves from living it, that is. That we could die before we are dead. That we could turn a loss, and a lesson, into a lifetime of pain. Because our cognitive function is making us think in such a way that keeps the impediment firmly in place. You know, where we never learn to act, even while in discomfort, and so we never move on.

When you're afraid, what you have to remember is that nothing presses us to release it unless something else is imminently waiting to arrive.

If the river weren't flowing from behind the impediment, then we wouldn't feel the pressure to allow it to come apart and release itself in time.

We think we build or choose the impetus of our lives—we find the person, the ideas, the opportunities—but in truth, we respond to them.

We don't force their arrival, because they are always en route. The doors are opening at every moment, but we have to choose what we walk through. And when the only door we are familiar with is fear, we often end up staying right where we are until we forget our ability to choose. We think that the only reality is the one we've known, not realizing that we've known so many different realities, we've had so many problems that we thought we'd never get over that do not even once pass through our minds today.

Remember that.

All the things you once obsessed over?

You thought about them one day for the very last time. And you didn't even know it was the last. And you were able to do that because…you kept going. And that is your living, breathing, personal proof…that you can get through this, too. That you can change. You can learn. You can use rock bottom as a clean slate. And that doesn't mean it's not going to hurt, it means you're now choosing to make something of the hurt. Because the hurt is kind of inevitable, we're human. But what's not inevitable is what we do with it.

Motion begets motion.

Momentum feeds upon itself.

Because momentum is actually a process of us lifting the impediments—both small and large—and allowing, allowing, allowing the flow.

It's far simpler than we think it is.

When we have a routine, in literally anything, we have an established set of actions that we have no impediments to, because we have practiced them without impairing their flow. Once we get used to it, the flow seems obvious, and even preferred. We begin to crave the feeling. And that's why, you know, routines can be so important and productive.

Anything that re-engages you with the real life act of living begins to lift the impediments to flow.

That's why brilliant ideas pop up from nothingness after a long walk. Why do we remember that thing we'd meant to do and suddenly feel the compulsion to do it after we've completed an unrelated but likewise important chore. That is why. Because we have begun to move ourselves out from beneath the illusion of stuck-ness and back into the nature of existing.

What you have to remember, in the end, is that the things that pose the hardest challenges to you are the ones that you are most meant to overcome.

And so every single time you think you are running up against a wall, hitting it again and again, and you will never see the other side—remember that your job is not to push through but to pioneer a new way around. To find a new way to the other side, and then to go there and be there.

Because the things you struggle with most are the ones you are here to master.

And the trail you leave behind in your own pursuit of your own self-actualization will become the guidelines for other people to do the same.

●

Fear is always built around what is untrue.
To overcome what you are afraid of, inquire:
"What falsehood is at the root of this?"

READ THIS WHEN YOU FEEL LIKE YOU HAVE TO ACCEPT ALL CRITICISM IN ORDER TO GROW

Do not take criticism from anyone you would not take advice from; do not take advice from anyone you wouldn't want to switch places with.

When you uphold the critic as being someone with a more potent opinion than the supporter, you are allowing that person to have a heavier hand in shaping your destiny.

The thing about the way other people will attempt to sabotage you is that they usually won't actually stand in front of you and prevent you from proceeding. Their strategies will take on a more covert and sinister approach. They will get you to stop yourself by planting enough seeds of doubt that you no longer think you *want* to go forward.

You will be stuck, but not because you are actually stuck.

You will have just grown to take more seriously the opinion of someone who probably does not want the best for you if it means they will no longer be able to rest their laurels on seeing the best in themselves.

This is not to say that you do not listen, or connect, or really attempt to understand anybody but those you admire, but that you begin to move forward with the understanding that those who have not traveled where you want to be do not yet have the roadmap to help you get there.

Real leadership—and artistic integrity, for that matter—is a process of both knowing who to listen to and then making informed decisions. To go first does not mean to go alone; it often really just means to be conscientious about who is influencing the nature of who you are becoming and not to listen to the calls from the sidelines as they ask, beg, or even at times threaten for you to conform to them. With intention, your life, and art, will become significant not only because you are living and creating in a way that differs from the average, but because you are doing it in a way that is more conscious than the norm.

Doing this will be a process of you learning who you are going to take most seriously.

Who cares about your well-being.

Who really loves you.

Who wants to see you win.

Who has no emotional investment in seeing you held back.

Who will be honest with you.

Who will tell you the full truth.

Who has already achieved the type of success you'd like to see in that particular domain of life.

Who has not, and therefore, can offer words of advice from a cautioned place.

But most of all, you will have to decide who you're going to admire, who you are going to allow to expand you, whose standards you will also adopt.

If you live your entire life attempting to mold yourself to the norms of those around you without any further consideration of whether or not those people are where you would one day like to be, you will end up exactly where they are. Stuck, frustrated, and wondering why the simplest acts of forward motion seem to bring with them the weight of a thousand opinions.

It is because they very often do.

Not everything projected onto you has something to do with you. Practice discernment. What you give authority to will shape the way the river of your life flows.

READ THIS WHEN YOU DON'T KNOW WHETHER TO HOLD ON OR LET GO

The right time to let go is always.

The second you begin to wonder whether or not it is time for you to open your palms and stop gripping is the exact moment that you should.

Because the things that are really right for you—the ones that resonate and land—they will remain. They will not require closed fists to keep them. They will not need you to tint them with a rose-colored lens. They will not ask you to list off all the reasons that make them right.

They will just be.

Letting go is not an event, it is a practice.

We learn how to do it with the small stuff, so when the big stuff comes, we are ready.

Letting go is not actually a matter of releasing or pushing away. It is a process of opening our hands and staying still and allowing things to show us their true nature. When we are no longer painting our love and hope and idealizations upon those things, we get to see what they actually are. From there, we get to choose.

The things we are most attached to—the things we most anxiously hold onto—are often the ones we sense, at some level, cannot be sustained on their own. That without our conscious participation, and filtering, and warming of them, they would not remain.

When you finally have the courage to stand in the quiet for a while, a new life often arrives to meet you at the doorway. You see things you hadn't before. You imagine things you didn't before. You try for things you wouldn't before. In that surrendered place, you begin to find your way back to yourself.

When you let go, you notice that the things that are right for you never leave you. They always return, clearer and stronger than they were before.

The only thing you're actually letting go of is the illusion that you will never find another door once you exit this one, when there is already an entirely new life knocking, asking you to find it, and begin.

The only thing you're actually letting go of is the idea that life was meant to just be lukewarm.

The only thing you're actually letting go is the assumption that you could not stand on your own, even for the briefest period of time.

The only thing you are letting go of is valuing how things appear behind other people's eyes over how they feel in your own heart.

The only thing you're actually letting go of is the false assumption that in place of what has gone, new and greater things could not arrive.

The only thing you're actually letting go of is the idea that all you'd ever deserve are the things that do not reach back.

•

Live with palms wide open—what's right will land and remain without your fists closing to keep it.

READ THIS WHEN YOU'VE LOST HOPE

Hope is not just when you think of all the good things ahead of you, but you remember the ones behind. You remember how far you've come. You remember how much has gone your way. You remember how much you've loved, how much you've seen, how much good you've done. You remember how much you've endured, how much you've let go of. You remember all of your tiny, heroic acts—even if only how you kept holding on, how you continued fighting, how you made it here today. You remember when you thought you couldn't put one foot in front of the other, and then all of the days when life felt so easy, and you felt so free, and how wrong you were about how hopeless it all seemed. You remember that the strength to take you forward was made through what got you here. You remember how perfect everything can be, because if you change what you choose to focus on, you change what you naturally see.

●

What you gather evidence for is what will appear most true. Gather evidence of your fortitude, your faith. Gather evidence of your strength, the way the road has always risen. If you don't trust ahead, look to what's behind. Remember, what got you here will get you to whatever's next.

READ THIS WHEN YOU'RE HOLDING YOURSELF BACK

If you could see your life in retrospect, if you could reverse engineer your regret, if you could imagine who you would be had you been fearless, had you realized what was in front of you all along—you would only wish you had made more of what you had while you still had it.

You would wish you had seen opportunity for what it was while it was still resting in the palm of your hand.

It's easy to find a sense of safety in withholding, as though not completely letting yourself into the experience would shelter you from its inevitable ending—whether that came before you anticipated, or a way you didn't want, or just by the virtue and nature of everything, which is temporary, even the most beautiful things of all. But abstaining does nothing. The feeling we get at the end of something we most fully give ourselves to is not a deeper regret but a deeper peace. We know that we did what we could with what we had, that we savored and made the most of it, that we tried, really tried. Often, the things we are unable to let go of and forgive ourselves for are the ones that we didn't fully live out. The desire still binds itself to us, making us fear that because the moment passed, so did the potential. It hasn't, though. The regret isn't trying to punish, it's trying to instruct. It's trying to say: there is still time to become who you always meant to.

Most of us live with a sense that the worst thing that could happen is that we fail, and what that failure would feel like, what it would mean about us, and how worthy we are or aren't as people. The actual worst thing that could happen is that we don't live while we are still alive and instead spend our years cycling through the same familiarities, all the while something deeper inside of us asks us to stretch, and open, and move toward something new.

The only thing you will look back and realize is that the entryways to the things you really wanted were always right beside you—you just had to find the courage to notice and leap.

If you are self-imposing limitation out of the assumption that shining too brightly will disturb the darkness within others, remember that in itself is an agreement to remain loyal to the dark. The more completely you are within your life, the more you will inspire others to re-enter their own arenas. Your light ricochets, refracts, and reminds.

READ THIS WHEN YOU DON'T KNOW WHAT TO DO NEXT

What assets do you have right now that you are not taking advantage of? What answered prayers are going unacknowledged, what glimmers of progress are going unrecognized? What little sparks of interest or possibility are attempting to grasp your attention, and which heavier weights of fear and decided failure are bearing down upon them and extinguishing your consideration before they have really been seen?

In what ways are you shortchanging your potential, in what ways have you taken yourself out of the arena before you were ever really in? In what ways are you guarding your heart by hurting it, as though you could safeguard by desensitizing, when your disproportionate focus upon the ways in which you might not be enough are scar tissuing them into your head enough to start fighting with your heart?

In what ways are you already playing dead?

If you could imagine that it was all taken away from you tomorrow, what would you most regret not being grateful for? Not seeing for what it was, while it was still there? In what ways are the doorways of opportunity outlining themselves along the closed walls of your perception, and what courage might you need to muster in order to realize that this very moment contains within it the unlikely entryway to what you've been asking for all along?

The next step is whatever is in front of you. The steps after will be revealed as you choose your path. To plan too intently is, in many ways, to limit what's possible, to limit what might be. Stay here, act now. The unfolding occurs in the infinite now.

READ THIS WHEN YOU FEEL LIKE YOU'RE HITTING YOUR UPPER LIMIT

When good things are trying to find you, I hope you let them. I hope that you leave room for things to turn out better than you had planned. I hope that you do not deny yourself happiness because you know how human you are, because you are most familiar with your rough edges, your mistakes, your past. I hope that when the sun is finally shining on you, you let yourself feel its warmth. I hope you don't think your way out of every beautiful thing that is trying to reach you. I hope you don't look back one day and realize that you were always the biggest thing standing in your own way.

I hope that you learn how to bring yourself home.

I hope you learn to differentiate comforting yourself with coddling; I hope you stop negotiating your standards down to your familiarities, I hope you stop talking yourself out of the person you actually want to be.

I hope that you will realize how often things meet you at your expectation of them. How presence is everything but you also have a choice in what moment you meet. How the way you set your gaze is often how you find the view. That you can decide, in any second of that infinite now, to look for the silver linings, the glimmers, the doorways that are cracked open, inviting you to see the possibility, the potential, the goodness that was always right there, waiting for you to see.

Most of all, I hope you will understand that you become the person you condition yourself to be. That you are a work of your own making, a nurturing that does not only happen by chance but also by choice. That more than anything else, you will become what you allow yourself to get used to, what you make normal, what you integrate into your hours in the most ordinary ways. I hope you will start to see how all those tiny gestures can add up to something far greater than their parts. I hope you will begin to realize the power you've always had deep inside, and how that power is actually resting in your capacity to choose in the smallest ways, until they become the biggest ones.

Your heart will forever be expanding and softening, allowing more beauty, wisdom, grace, and experience inside of it. Allow it to stretch. Don't assume the place where your discomfort starts is where your possibility ends. In many ways, it's right where it is beginning.

READ THIS WHEN YOU FEEL STUCK OR AS THOUGH NOTHING WILL EVER CHANGE

Rumi told us that the wound is the place where the light can enter. Khalil Gibran told us that out of suffering emerges the strongest souls, that the most massive characters are seared with scars. Marcus Aurelius told us that the impediment to action advances action, that what stands in the way becomes the way. Napoleon Hill told us that every adversity, every failure, and every heartache carries with it the seeds of an equal or greater benefit.

Elisabeth Kübler-Ross told us that the most beautiful people we have known are those "who have known defeat, known suffering, known struggle, known loss, and have found their way out of the depths. These persons have an appreciation, a sensitivity, and an understanding of life that fills them with compassion, gentleness, and a deep loving concern."

That "beautiful people do not just happen."

When Joseph Campbell outlined the hero's journey for us, the premise was that at the moment of the deepest and most unmoving difficulty, the protagonist recognized that it was they who must change. That which seemed to derail the path was the pinnacle moment at which the true path was actually revealed.

In each case, the epiphany is that the presence of the challenge is the initiator. If we are lucky, our lives will continue to grow as we are presented with new paths and various obstacles among them. To heal is not to arrive at a place where we are absolved of that difficulty, but where we no longer interpret the presence of it as our finality, our ending. Rather, we come to see it as yet another beginning in support of the continual unfolding of all we will one day know ourselves to be.

In a world where most of us die before we are dead, where most of us hyper-fixate on what we cannot control and leave in ruins everything that we can, where most of us fear our humanness and our vulnerability—I hope you find the courage to try. I hope you will come to see that just maybe, beneath the journey you fear to take is the life you had been waiting for all along.

Growth is what happens when the selves we once were reach a threshold where they can no longer carry us forward, and in their place, new and truer selves must emerge and form. When we effortlessly adapt, the process feels easy. When the old parts of ourselves that were constructed in response to fear and trauma resist their own alchemy, what rises within us is this sense of panic and disarray, and if we are not careful, it is the very moment where we are most at risk of adopting the most limiting beliefs of all: that what is most familiar to us is most correct for us; that who we have been is who we will always be.

It is less important to ask "Who am I?" than it is to ask: "Who would I like to be?"

Who you think you are is very often just who you've had to be. In some ways, that's the truth of all of us—a patchwork of everyone and everything we've known, loved, seen, and done. But we are also amendable, and as much as the outside world has nurtured our sense of truth, so can our internal ones. We are, in larger ways than not, of our own making.

That is the most empowering notion and also the most terrifying. There is no more defaulting in this acceptance. There is no more looking around and blaming or holding on. There is only the choice of whether we will hurt to stay as we've been or hurt to become who we might be. There is no workaround for discomfort, the shadows are rendered by the light. What we get to decide is what we're going to endure for. What our greater intention will be. What we are going to let ourselves get used to. What we are going to reorient our comfort zones around so often and so honestly that in time, we become known to the world as we only ever once imagined ourselves to be.

Growth is when we let go of the known parts of ourselves—the accepted, the understood, the comfortable parts—in favor of building new ones. Parts that give us the inner sense of openness to love where we were once closed, respond where we once only reacted, choose where we once felt it was chosen for us, and become a kind of person that only once seemed viable in our wildest dreams.

You aren't stuck. The reality you are experiencing is not one in which you are actually encumbered by your stagnancy, but rather, anchored by attachment to what's ready to pass away, what's ready to transform, what's ready to be different than it was before. Feeling as though you're between a metaphorical rock and a hard place is actually you recognizing that a new part of your story is ready to be written, but you are still deeply entrenched in the narrative you had running before.

The irony is that the very moments when we are most convinced nothing is moving in our favor are usually the same points at which everything is ready to.

You wouldn't be able to recognize the part of you that's stuck if there wasn't another part of you that had already become free.

•

You are a being in constant flow, constant flux. Everything is changing, even if it appears as though it is all staying still. Learn to meet the day not with an assumption of what it will be, but a curiosity of what could unfold. Within that simple shift, you'll find entire universes that want to reveal themselves to you. Entire pieces of you that have been ready and waiting to come to be.

READ THIS WHEN YOU FEEL LIKE EVERYTHING IS FALLING APART

This is your sign that there are pieces of your life coming together right now that are bigger than you can see. That in the movements and changes and adjustments that feel so scary, so disappointing, so disconcerting, you are being intricately guided to exactly where you've asked, and envisioned, and worked so hard to be.

You have not been forgotten.

You are not falling behind.

In fact, this is the moment when things are most coming together.

The beautiful thing is also the hard one—that sometimes, we have to compromise what's comfortable for what's true. That we can grow so accustomed to the things that are not quite right for us, we can begin to confuse them for certainty, for home. That we could grow and wind roots around what was only meant to be temporary—a lesson, a learning period—and break our own hearts in the process of saving our souls.

But those hearts are resilient, and they're made even more so when we realize that the things we are most attached to are blank canvases upon which we have painted our love and made them good. And that quality, that ability, goes with us wherever we are. It only grows as it learns, as it begins to discern, as it stumbles back into the things that are so undeniably right, so clearly meant for us.

And those things that are so undeniably right and clearly meant? They aren't that way because we find them and they are instantaneously perfect, but because the ground is clear enough and the perimeter is wide enough and the open possibility matches the vision we have of what it could be—and so we begin and we continue.

If we do not give up, we build the things we most want, from the inside out.

So when life seems to be redirecting you—when the changes are swift and sudden, especially—remember that you have no idea what future pain your current discomfort is saving you from. Particularly when you consider that there is no greater regret than getting to the end of your days and realizing that you wasted your time; you did not do what you came here to do.

The minute it feels like some things are falling apart is the same minute others are attempting to come together. Trust how life wants to unfold. It's all for you. It's all for you.

BRIANNA WIEST is the bestselling author of the books *101 Essays That Will Change The Way You Think, The Mountain Is You, The Pivot Year,* and more. Her books have sold millions of copies, regularly appear on global bestseller lists, and are currently being translated into 40+ languages. She has a B.A. in English and an Honorary Doctorate in Literature from Elizabethtown College. She lives and works in Northern California and travels to speak at businesses, conferences, and bookstores worldwide.

briannawiest.com
instagram.com/briannawiest
facebook.com/briannawiestauthor
x.com/briannawiest

Please send all inquiries to info@briannawiest.com

THOUGHT CATALOG Books

Thought Catalog Books is a publishing imprint of Thought Catalog, a digital magazine for thoughtful storytelling, and is owned and operated by The Thought & Expression Co. Inc., an independent media group based in the United States of America. Founded in 2010, we are committed to helping people become better communicators and listeners to engender a more exciting, attentive, and imaginative world. The Thought Catalog Books imprint connects Thought Catalog's digital-native roots with our love of traditional book publishing. The books we publish are designed as beloved art pieces. We publish work we love. Pioneering an author-first and holistic approach to book publishing, Thought Catalog Books has created numerous best-selling print books, audiobooks, and eBooks translated into 40+ languages.

ThoughtCatalog.com | **Thoughtful Storytelling**

ShopCatalog.com | **Shop Books + Curated Products**

MORE FROM
BRIANNA WIEST

When You're Ready, This Is How You Heal

*101 Essays That Will Change
The Way You Think*

The Mountain Is You

I Am The Hero Of My Own Life

The Pivot Year

Ceremony

Salt Water

Shop books and products
by the author at **shopcatalog.com.**

MORE FROM
THOUGHT CATALOG BOOKS

The Art Of Who We Are
Robert W. Dean

Emotional Aesthetics
Ashley Klassen

It Is All Equally Fragile
Alison Malee

The Words We Left Behind
Callie Byrnes

Moments To Hold Close
Molly Burford

The Unbearable Beauty
Poems and Practices for Being Alive
Annabelle Blythe

Face Yourself. Look Within.
Adrian Michael

All The Right Pieces
Nakeia Homer

THOUGHT CATALOG Books

THOUGHTCATALOG.COM

On the other side of the life you are trying to keep together, on the other side of the pain you think will never dissolve into peace, on the other side of everything you are forcing—is the life that is waiting.

The life where you are not pushed by your fears but moved by your vision. The life where the right things arrive and remain, and you do not have to contort your truth to make them so. The life where you are actually living, not just waiting to begin. The life that is really yours. The life you arrive to the end of with tired eyes and a full heart. The life that you are proud of. The life that you actually want. The life that is gently asking you to let go and see it.

The life that's been waiting, all this time, for you to arrive.

THOUGHT CATALOG Books